OTHER TITLES PUBLISHED BY TEXAS FISH & GAME PUBLISHING CO., LLC

Books:

Saltwater Strategies®: Texas Trout Tactics
by Chester Moore, Jr.

Saltwater Strategies®: Flounder Fever
by Chester Moore, Jr.

Saltwater Strategies®:
Pat Murray's No-Nonsense Guide to Coastal Fishing
by Pat Murray

Texas Saltwater Classics:
Fly Patterns for the Texas Coast
by Greg Berlocher

Kayak Texas
by Greg Berlocher

Saltwater Strategies®: Wade Fish Texas
by Bink Grimes

101 Freshwater Launching Sites for Kayak Fishing
by Paul Batchelder, Sr.

Doreen's 24 Hour Eat Gas Now Café
by Reavis Z. Wortham

Periodicals:

Texas Fish & Game Magazine

Texas Lakes & Bays Atlas (annual)

For information, contact us at:

281-869-5511

www.fishgame.com

Texas Fish & Game Publishing Co., LLC
3431 Rayford Rd Suite 200-408
Spring, Texas 77386
281-869-5511

Texas Fish & Game's

SALTWATER STRATEGIES®

BOOK SERIES PRESENTS

By Chester Moore, Jr.

TEXAS FISH & GAME PUBLISHING CO., L.L.C.

3431 Rayford Rd Suite 200-408

Spring, Texas 77386

281-869-5511

Online: www.fishgame.com

Published by

Texas Fish & Game Publishing Co., L.L.C.

3431 Rayford Rd Suite 200-408
Spring, Texas 77386
Phone: 281-869-5511
Website: www.fishgame.com

Revised Edition

Cover photo by George Knighten

Foreword by Ed Holder

Edited by Don Zaidle

All photos by Chester Moore, Jr., unless otherwise credited.

Production design by Wendy Kipfmiller

Layout by Doug Berry

ISBN: 978-0-9908415-2-4

DEDICATION

This book is dedicated to my daughter Faith. I love you more than you could know and hope this book and my body of work makes you proud. You are forever my little Panda Bear.

Chester Moore, Jr.

Contents

Foreword

A Fishy Writer

Readers of this and other books written by Chester Moore might wonder if he is a writer/fisherman or fisherman/writer. That's a difficult question to answer because he's a writer who loves to fish and a fisherman who loves to write. One thing is clear, however: the two loves have produced a writer who knows his subject.

Chester grew up a bicycle ride from coastal estuaries where redfish roamed. He was introduced to these bullies of brackish water at an early age and has been chasing them ever since. That chase has carried him from his bicycle waters to many coastal bays and out into the Gulf of Mexico and taught him much about redfish.

He shares his knowledge in this book. He does it with an easy-going style anglers can understand and appreciate, whether they are inexperienced beginners or "old salts"; whether they have expensive boating rigs or do their fishing from the bank; whether they like to feed redfish various baits or fool them with lures. He even offers some proven recipes for cooking redfish, and digs into conservation issues important to those who like to catch redfish. He also does it with the enthusiasm of a dedicated fisherman—and writer. There I go again. But you decide after reading the book. Is he a writer/fisherman or fisherman/writer?

—Ed Holder

(Ed Holder passed away in 2005 but had the opportunity to write this foreword just before the first edition of this book went to press. He was without question of the greatest writers and redfish angler ever on the Gulf Coast.)

Introduction
Growing Up Fishing

"Big John!"

Utter those words to any of the kids in my old neighborhood in West Orange, Texas around 1984 and they would either burst with excitement or shiver in fear. Big John was a very polarizing character you see.

Looking back, that is an impressive feat for an alligator garfish that allegedly lived in a tiny branch of Adams Bayou that crossed under Newton Street we simply called the "The Gully".

Big John was very much like Bigfoot as sighting reports traveled quickly and the eyewitnesses met with a mixture of skepticism and fanfare.

Claiming you saw Big John would garner you a following among the dozen or so boys in the neighborhood and jeers from the girls who all thought we were off our rockers for pursuing such a thing if it did indeed exist.

This gully is where I spent much of my after school time and during summer vacation. And while the fishing was rarely outstanding; we did catch our fair share of spotted gar, grinnel, sun perch and mud cats.

At times, it was quite the social gathering as it was common for at least half a dozen of us to be wetting our lines and talking about whatever the current hot topic was.

One day it might be whether Gene Simmons from Kiss really had a cow's tongue implanted to replace his own so he could look cool wagging it onstage and the next it could be a heated debate over who was going to win the title at the next Wrestlemania.

The conversation, however, would always drift to Big John and his latest exploits.

One kid swore to have seen him attack a calf that came to drink on the water's edge while another claimed to have had his rod broken by the beast on three occasions. None of these occurrences ever happened when we were together, but no one questioned them aloud.

The stories gave us something to talk about and looking back, a unique means of bonding.

I never had an official sighting but once a kid named Joey was fishing with a hand line from the bridge that crossed the gully. I was on the other side of the road with two big lines set out when I heard frantic splashing in the water.

Joey was clinging on to his line and as I rushed over to see what was going on, his line snapped. I could see a large, dark shape move through the water as whatever it was swam off with Joey's bait. That could have been many things, but of course, we thought Big John had struck again.

As time passed on, our interest in fishing at the gully waned along with banter of Big John.

Chasing girls, high school sports and fast cars now dominated the lives of the boys in my part of West Orange. For a while, I would still occasionally fish down there, but when I got a car, it made more sense to drive out to Sabine Lake or the Neches River. The angling prospects were vastly superior there. We will get to than in serious fashion here shortly.

PHOTO BY GEORGE KNIGHTEN

Spotting a "tailing" redfish is one of the most thrilling experiences on the Gulf Coast

Recently, I drove by that gully on the way to my parent's house and stopped for a brief look. Now, there is a "No Fishing" sign on the bridge and there were no kids there angling for garfish and dreams. No matter what happened in our lives, we always found sanctuary down at the gully fishing for Big John. Wealthy, poor and middle class kids got along just fine with our attentions focused on finding our own white whale of sorts in this murky East Texas bayou branch.

As I drove off, I adjusted my rear-view mirror and caught a glimpse of a large splash in the water. It was probably a school of mullet or perhaps one of the resident alligators playing around.

I would however like to think it was Big John, out on the hunt and making some commotion to say hello to an old friend. I would like to think that very much.

Those early days were formative in my love of the outdoors. The gully provided so many fun experiences and lessons that taught me much about fishing and in my life I have been blessed to have some amazing fishing encounters.

A story of a giant garfish might seem an unusual way to open introduce a book on redfish. While, I have never been one to stick with convention.

But the truth is this love of fishing and the time we spent at that gully have a lot to do with redfish. Back then it was nearly impossible to catch a keeper-sized redfish and giant bull reds were nearly nonexistent. We were coming out of a long period of commercial harvest where redfish had nearly been decimated and I remember we kids would talk about redfish as if they were blue marlin.

Our shortness gar, grinned and mud cats kept us happy but we fantasized about catching redfish, especially the fabled "bull reds" that reportedly hit so hard they would break large surf rods.

I have always regarded redfish in high esteem and maybe it was because early on they seemed unreachable.

Redfish are beautiful, fight hard, and have some of the tastiest flesh in the sea. Some of my earliest childhood memories are of rolling redfish in cracker meal for family fish fries. I can almost taste the golden brown fillets delighting my taste buds, along with homemade French fries and coleslaw. Redfish fries were a family tradition and one that carries on to this day, the only difference being Dad now delegates me to cleaning duties while he gets the comfortable battering gig.

Tradition is something that surrounds redfish more than any inland game species. I admit that flounder are my favorite saltwater sport fish, and speckled trout get more attention from the outdoor media, but redfish have a certain aura about them. A powerful, nostalgic vibe goes along with pursuing them.

This is the second edition of this book and we have added chapters, expanded others and updated information and photos. It was exciting to revisit this book I wrote so long ago and it makes me quite happy that today redfish are doing great not only in my home state of Texas but also throughout the Gulf Coast region.

I hope you enjoy this book and I truly believe it will help you catch more and bigger redfish—you know that kind that easily snap rods into two.

Well, those stories might have been exaggerated by us young anglers back in the 80s but there is no question redfish fight hard, taste good and give millions of anglers on the Gulf Coast big thrills.

Thank God for the redfish!

Chapter One

Life of the Redfish

The red drum, *Sciaenops ocellatus*, is a fish of many monikers. Most anglers in Texas and Louisiana call it "redfish", but some call it "channel bass" in parts of Florida, and "*pescado colorado*" or simply "*colorado*" in Mexico.

Redfish, as I will identify them throughout this book, also get names for different age classes. "Rat red" signifies juveniles whereas the term "bull red" applies to big, sexually mature specimens.

As a kid, I used to get a real kick out of the tag "channel bass" because I had a Lone Star Beer "Saltwater Fish of Texas" poster that had that name listed under the redfish. To this day, I cannot figure where the "bass" part came in. They look nothing like a largemouth (assuming the namer had that species in mind), and their fight puts to shame anything from freshwater of comparable size.

The best description I have found for the physical traits and habits of the species is from a study entitled: "The Red Drum in Texas" by James A. Dailey, Coastal Fisheries Division, Texas Parks & Wildlife Department (TPWD).

> The red drum is a member of the drum family whose cousins include the Atlantic croaker, spot, spotted seatrout, and black drum. The most distinguishing mark on the red drum is one large black spot on the upper part of the tail base. Having multiple spots is not uncommon for this fish but having no spots is extremely rare. The color of red drum ranges from a deep blackish, coppery color to nearly silver. The most common color is reddish-bronze.

I disagree with that last sentence. A redfish is bronze, but I cannot find any red to them at all. We should call them "bronzefish." That would make a lot more sense, but what do I know?

The species is fast growing, reaching approximately 11 inches and 1 pound in its first year, 17-22 inches and 3-1/2 pounds in two years, and 22-24 inches and 6-8 pounds in three years. The world record red drum weighed 96 pounds and hailed from the East coast. The current Texas record is 55 pounds.

> Red drum reach sexual maturity between their third and fourth years when they are about thirty inches long. They spawn in the Gulf, possibly near the mouths of passes. On the Texas coast spawning occurs generally from mid-August through mid-October. Eggs hatch within 24 hours and are carried into the bays by tidal current. The larval red drum seeks quiet, shallow water with grassy or muddy bottoms.

For the first three years, redfish live in the bays or in the surf zone near passes and jetties. Evidence from TPWD's tag returns show that they remain

Redfish feed on everything from blue crabs to mullet pictured here. Mullet is one of the standby baits for reds.

in the same area and generally move less than three miles from where fisheries officials tag them. I know this firsthand.

In June 2001, while fishing the Texas side of the Sabine jetties with Bill Killian of Orange, Texas, I caught a redfish that I had tagged more than three weeks earlier at the cluster of rigs located just east of the jetties. I was hoping other anglers would catch some of the fish I had tagged, but never thought *I* would.

Nasty green algae covered the tag, but it was easy to read after I wiped it off. The tag's number was 31. The big red was caught and released like all others that day and perhaps to be caught again by another angler. The chances of catching one's own tagged fish has to be minuscule, but it proved these fish do not move much.

> As they mature, they move from the bays to the Gulf of Mexico where they remain the rest of their lives, except for infrequent visits to the bays. Although there is little evidence of seasonal migrations, anglers find concentrations of red drum in rivers and tidal creeks during the winter. Daily movement from the shallows to deeper waters is influenced by tides and water temperatures.

During the fall, especially during stormy weather, large adult red drum move to the Gulf beaches, possibly for spawning, where they can be caught from piers and by surf anglers. Anglers call this the "bull redfish run."

Juvenile redfish feed mainly on small crab, shrimp, and marine worms. As they mature, they move on to larger crab, shrimp, and small fish. They are designed to feed on the bottom, but will feed anywhere in the water column when the opportunity arises. In a later chapter, you will read about the incredible phenomenon of schooling redfish where hundreds of them gather and destroy anything in their path. Sometimes this happens in 50 feet of water in the Gulf of Mexico, and at other times in super shallow areas.

Another phenomenon is "tailing," which involves the reds' tails sticking out of the water as they feed in the shallows. In some areas, anglers should call this "backing" because you see a lot more back and dorsal fin than spotted tail at a 45-degree angle. Either way, it is bad ass in my book.

Redfish prefer salty areas, but do just fine in pure freshwater marsh. In fact, my late mentor, Ed Holder, would sight-cast to them in an area where they swam with channel catfish and largemouth bass.

TPWD has successfully stocked them in several freshwater reservoirs including Fairfield, Braunig, and Calaveras. They cannot spawn in these lakes, but they grow to immense size and take to the habitat like, well, a fish takes to water. Instead of feeding on crab, they eat crawfish and terrorize the perch, shad, bass, and other wimpy freshwater species.

Redfish are highly adaptable, and this allows them to survive in many habitats and live to great age. According to the North Carolina Department of Environment and Fisheries, the oldest recorded specimen was 62 years old, caught in the Atlantic Ocean.

Ocean-going redfish are still a mystery to scientists. As detailed previously, the juveniles are supposed to spend their first three years inshore, but anglers routinely catch juveniles offshore. I have caught reds in the 20 to 28-inch class as far as 40 miles offshore. This obviously represents a segment of the population scientists have not figured out yet, and that puts them in the same boat

The barnacle-encrusted structure of oil platforms is a magnet for big bull redfish.

with anglers.

This book has many tips for catching these highly sporting fish, but as any dedicated pursuer of redfish knows, they always have a surprise up their gills.

Chapter Two

Seasonal Patterns & Tactics:

The beautiful thing about redfish is anglers can catch them with relative ease throughout the year. The biggest segment of the flounder population leaves the bays during winter, and speckled trout simply get lockjaw, but it seems like redfish are always biting somewhere.

I remember freezing my butt off while fishing off the side of the road with my dad during the winter catching one redfish after another. People thought we were crazy, but winter is a great time to catch reds—and so are spring, summer, and fall.

Let's look at the best tactics and locations for redfish throughout the seasons.

SPRING

Redfish dwell in shallow areas year-round. During certain times of year, they take to the main water or inhabit deep areas in ship channels, but there are always reds in the shallows. Target springtime reds around shorelines adjacent to cuts in the marshes and along mud flats. In the early part of March, the water is still rather cool and shallow mud flats near deep water, like ship channels, hold many reds on warm, sunny afternoons. The black mud holds heat, which brings in baitfishes, which in turn bring in reds.

Oyster reefs are one of the most overlooked areas to target redfish during spring. That may be because understanding and fishing oyster reefs is complex. Anglers have to consider everything from depth, tidal movement, and predator-prey relations to water clarity and the all-important influx of freshwater.

Bay systems are prone to flooding in the spring. The flooding, in fact, can get so bad that surface water miles out into the Gulf of Mexico can be almost purely fresh.

Redfish are very tolerant of freshwater, but they typically concentrate in heavier numbers in saltwater during flooded periods. Saltwater is heavier than freshwater so it goes to the bottom and that is where the redfish will be. The deepest water will be the saltiest water, and in ecosystems like Galveston Bay many of the oyster reefs are in deep water. Reefs on the southern end of bays are especially good places to look for redfish because they have a strong tidal flow, which brings in saltier water from the Gulf. During spring floods, oyster reefs covered by deep water are loaded with redfish.

Oyster reefs are unique ecosystems. In open, barren bay systems typical of Texas, they are like an oasis in the desert. They are great spots for small baitfishes to seek refuge and prey on microorganisms. This is turn makes them great places to contact opportunistic predators like redfish.

Oyster reefs harbor your typical batfishes like mullet, menhaden, glass minnows, and crab, but they also attract some unusual species. Sand eels are one of the most prolific baitfish species that inhabit oyster reefs, and they are a favorite prey item of redfish. This is especially true during April, when the menhaden are small, and shrimp are hard to find. It is a rare occurrence to catch a redfish during this time that does not have sand eels in its belly. This should be a clue to anglers.

Beginning in early summer one of the most exciting things for anglers on the Gulf Coast to do is attempt to catch a tagged redfish in CCA's STAR tournament. Tagged reds lead anglers to very special prizes.

The Norton Sand Eel is a great sand eel imitator. This bait has come on strong in the last couple of years, and comes in a variety of colors for various water conditions and personal preferences. During drought years, cutlass fish, also known as ribbonfish, are common on oyster reefs and redfish will absolutely gorge themselves on them. Drift with the current and let the lure bounce, bump, and crash into the oyster reef. Water conditions during spring usually

"Wild" Bill Skinner hoists two massive redfish he caught while fishing with the author at the Sabine Jetties. Actually, the author caught one and he caught the other at the same time.

range from off-colored to murky to just plain nasty, so anything that might grab the attention of a redfish is worth trying.

Make sure you have enough line out so that you are not fishing vertically. The lure will not work properly that way. In addition, it is important to keep contact with the lure. Springtime redfish are not overly aggressive and often hit soft plastic lures lightly. Use a super sensitive monofilament or braided line for best results.

It is important to remember that Mother Nature did not create equal oyster reefs, and she did not make reefs just one big, flat block of oysters. You want to look for structure within the structure. An oyster reef is a structure all by itself, but there is structure on top of that structure. A big clump of oysters rising up on a slight ridge on a reef with an average depth of 10 feet is structure on structure. A sunken boat on a reef is structure on structure.

It is very important to keep watch for drop-offs. A ledge that drops off to 16 feet on a 10 feet deep reef is a hot fishing spot. These are the places redfish gang up to intercept baitfishes. If you just jump over these spots without letting out extra line, you may not reach the fish. Keep your electronics on and look for the drop-off. When you hit it, let out some extra line and you will probably catch fish.

An indispensable tool in reef fishing is a marker buoy. You can purchase them at a tackle store or simply make your own with 2-liter cola bottles. When coming across a hotspot, throw out the buoys so you can return there. There

PHOTO BY GEORGE KNIGHTEN

Anglers should photograph exposed structure like this oyster reef during periods of low tide so they can better fish them when the tide is high.

might be 200 fish bunched up in a 20-yard spot, and that may be where they stay all day. You must be able to stay within the bite window to be successful.

SUMMER

Calm, slick days mean schooling redfish during summer. I have dedicated an entire chapter to fishing for schooling redfish elsewhere in this book, but it is worth brief mention here. Schooling reds are one of the most magnificent sights this outdoor writer has ever seen—and I have fished everywhere from Venezuela to Venice, Louisiana. These reds gather by the acre in the nearshore Gulf of Mexico and in the bays. The largest school I have seen covered an area of about three acres; redfish were everywhere.

It does not take rocket science to find these fish. When they are feeding on top, they look like a nuclear submarine rising from the abyss. Moreover,

Diana Suire caught this huge bull redfish in the surf during the heat of summer.

PHOTO BY GEORGE KNIGHTEN

Sand-eel imitators like the Bass Assassin are killer for redfish.

when they are just cruising around, the water around them takes on a glorious bronze tint.

"One thing that happens when people get into the big bull reds is, they usually end up wearing themselves out," said Capt. Tim Bradbeer, a Texas bull redfish specialist. "They got so excited catching the first few fish, and then after a half dozen or so, their muscles are aching, but they love every minute of it. I guarantee that."

Targeting redfish in the marsh is another viable option during summer. Look for reds along grassy shorelines and in areas where a hard bottom meets soft bottom. The best way to locate such areas without getting in the water and feeling around is to look for Roseau cane. It grows on harder bottoms, so the area around it is a prime place to hunt reds. Roseau cane's rooting system holds lots of crabs and that is a redfish favorite.

In super shallow water, look for "tailing" redfish, which are simply reds with their tails sticking out of the water. As detailed in the topwater chapter, cast directly in front of redfish for the best chance of getting a strike. Topwaters and spoons are the best lures for this practice.

Besides catching them schooling, my favorite way to find summer reds is at night. Look for shallow flats adjacent to deep water. These flats hold lots of baitfishes at night, which attracts reds. Crab is the best bait for redfish in these areas. Broken in half and hooked through the carapace, crab has a long hook life and is irresistible to reds. Squid is sometimes used, as is jumbo shrimp, but my favorite is live croaker. Live croaker is better for offshore, but it works in bays as well. The usual drill involves throwing a couple of rods out in the flats and then one in the nearby deep water. The shallows produce most of the fish, but occasionally the deep gives up a trophy-sized fish.

FALL

Bull redfish excite me, and I do not care who knows it. As I have written in *Texas Fish & Game* magazine and other publications, the big, beautiful bronze beasts stir my soul with each glorious encounter. There is something about them that hits me at a spiritual level.

This dates back to the first time I ever saw one at Meacom's Pier on the Bolivar Peninsula. As the full moon shined over the calm, clear surf, I noticed a hint of bronze in the water. It was massive bull red swimming under the lights of the pier. For years, I had heard the tales of hard-fighting, gigantic redfish, but this was my first-ever personal encounter. To a youngster who obsessed over such things, it was like coming face to face with a legend. I was in love.

After that first red appeared, it did not take long for others to join it and cause line alarms to sing send fishermen rushing to their rods. I stood amidst the excitement and prayed I would feel the same many more times. I craved an encounter with a bull redfish then, and I crave one now.

Fortunately, there are plenty of opportunities to encounter these prized sport fish on the Texas coast during the fall months. They have made a strong comeback since the government stopped commercial harvest more than 20 years ago, and pier fishing is not just viable but highly productive. Most pier anglers use lengthy surf rods that allow for long distance casting. These are especially helpful to anglers who do not like crowded piers and prefer the solace

This nice Lake Calcasieu red fell to a topwater thrown along a protected shoreline.

of lonely surf. A surf rod helps them get their bait past the first couple of sandbars. Do not be afraid to go after reds on piers if you do not have a surf rod. I have seen several anglers land reds on tackle ranging from Penn Senators rigged on short offshore sticks to an Ambassadeur 6500 attached to a popping rod. If you are proficient at playing big fish, you should be able to land a red on most any gear. Just set your drag accordingly.

Should you choose to fish areas of the surf where there are no piers, look for structure. Structure is the key to locating the greatest concentration of fish. Just setting up on a stretch of beach because it looks pretty will not necessarily be productive for bull redfish. The first thing to look for is points. The classic point configuration extends out at right angles to the beach. Sometimes the beach curves and it may look more like a "bend," but this is still a point. Sometimes, small submerged points are practically invisible to the naked eye, but anglers can spot them by looking for small "rips" close to the beach. It is usually best to fish the water sweeping past points or right at the tip. Other good point-related locations include the sloping sides, which anglers sometimes call "pockets" because they appear as scooped out impressions from the base of a point on both sides. Pockets often hold many crustaceans, which in turn draw in redfish.

Bowls are another kind of structure to look for when searching for fish in the surf. Bowls indent into the shore and form between two points. They are usually subtler than a point, but can still hold tremendous numbers of redfish. I have little experience fishing for redfish in the surf, but have had success on a couple of occasions at a deep bowl located near High Island.

Troughs are the most commonly mentioned structure in the surf-fishing game. They are simply impressions that run parallel to sand bars and provide means for fish to travel down the surf. Fish tend to feed along the sides of a trough rather than in its center, especially in spots where the trough drops off steeply from shallow water. Find these spots and you will usually find fish.

Piers and surf are fine places to catch bull reds, but there is no better place than at the jetty systems that lead into Texas bays and the nearshore Gulf. Jetties draw redfish in like a moth to flame and are easy to pattern, especially during fall. For anglers new to jetty fishing, I will keep it simple.

To catch bull reds at the jetties, find the deep holes on the Gulf or ship channel side. These holes will hold as many redfish as you can handle. I have caught as many as 15 of the brutes in one hole at the Sabine jetties, and had similar success at Galveston and Surfside. The best spot to look is at the southern tip of the jetty where it opens up to the Gulf. The current causes deep washouts where the wall divides the Gulf and ship channel. These spots are usually loaded with reds. Another good spot is the boat cut, which provide a strong tidal exchange and a buffet of crab and baitfishes.

In the nearshore Gulf out to a couple of miles, it is possible to encounter schooling bull redfish. I have seen schools as large as an Academy store parking

PHOTO BY MARK DAVIS

The author caught this nice red using a Bomber Saltwater Grade Super Pogy. A grip like the one pictured here can help when removing treble hooks and avoid a trip to the hospital and lots of pain.

lot. You will notice these schools because they make about as much commotion as a surfacing nuclear submarine. It is a beautiful sight. These schooling reds will hit just about anything you throw at them, but I would advise live croaker or mullet along with 1/2-ounce silver spoons and Rat-L-Traps. As I noted previously, these schooling reds can be spooky. I find them even more so in the fall. They may seem fearless as they madly thrash the surface, but they are actually a very spooky fish. If you see schooling reds, cut your motor a long way from them and switch over to your trolling motor. If the reds go under, approach the area where you last saw them and begin drifting. Sometimes they will follow the current to catch up with whatever they are feeding on, so drifting is a good way to find them without spooking. Starting up the big motor could mess things up.

Another option is the nearshore oil and gas platforms off the coast They rigs are stacked with oversized redfish during fall, and many of them are located within state waters where the government allows you to possess redfish. Keeping reds is illegal in federal waters of the Gulf of Mexico.

My favorite bull redfish bait is live croaker, hands down, without a doubt. Cut mullet fished on the bottom is also a good way to bag these redfish, but sometimes they seem to prefer suspended bait. In this case, fish with a mullet or whole blue crab on a free-line. I frequently catch bull reds this way on the same setup I use for sharks in the summer. I use a 4-foot steel leader finished off with a Daiichi Tru-Turn hook. The leader offers some protection from the pilings of the rigs and the circle hook allows me to catch and release big reds without harming them; most of the time, the circle hook lodges in the corner of the red's mouth. If you have never used circle hooks, I would recommend placing the rod in a holder and allowing the fish to hook itself. Do not try to set the hook as you would with a regular J-style hook. After the rod starts bending, over give it a slight tug and start reeling in. You will actually catch more fish this way than you will would with a j style-hook.

Using chum can greatly aid catching big redfish. Most anglers do not utilize chum when seeking reds, but I have found it very useful. I always hang a lingerie bag filled with mashed menhaden over the side to attract fish.

To catch these massive reds on lures, a 1-ounce gold spoon chunked toward the platform legs can be a real killer. Throw out about 10 feet from the leg and let it slowly flutter down.

No matter where you catch them, something to keep in mind with bull reds is they are highly stressed after a vigorous battle. If you plan to release it, get it back in the water as soon as possible. When fishing from a pier, use a drop net to bob the fish up and down to help get some oxygen going through its gills. In addition, check to see if the fish has a distended air bladder. If so, pop it with a fillet knife or other sharp object. This will help increase the chances of survival.

To take slot-size redfish, target the main body of the bay and look for them feeding under birds. It will be difficult to tell whether reds or trout are feeding, but either way you cannot lose. When the big blue northers come through, look to the cuts emptying the marsh to produce the most redfish. When the water leaves the marsh, so does everything that lives there, and this creates a buffet for big reds. Look for slight drop-offs just outside of cuts to hold the most redfish.

WINTER

Finding big concentrations of redfish in winter can be tough. Fish are cold-blooded and do not really like winter. They seek sanctuary from winter weather, which is why warm water outfall canals are such great fishing holes. Along the Texas coast, there are several warm water discharges from energy plants and refineries that can harbor incredible numbers of fish.

I grew up fishing around the Entergy Plant near Bridge City. It is like several similar outfits along the Texas Gulf Coast in that it cools its turbines by pumping water from one canal and expelling it into another. In this case, the water is coming from a marsh bordering the Lower Neches Wildlife Management Area and is exiting into a canal that leads to the mouth of the Neches River. Both usually hold salty water during winter. Baitfishes congregate in such warm waters during cold spells, making a buffet for a host of large predators. They are great for human predators, too, since the cold-blooded fish become more active feeders in these warm spots.

Warm-water discharges come in many forms. They can be a huge cooling plant that spews out thousands of gallons of warm water a minute, or they can be a small drainage pipe or culvert that has a very light flow. Chemical refineries often have small pump stations that produce warm water flow that diverts into underwater pipes.

Any of these areas can hold a surprising amount of fish. The more flow and the warmer the water compared to the surrounding waters, the more fish there will be. An interesting phenomenon in these areas is that different species favor various degrees of warmth or current. For example, redfish congregate next to the outflow pipes and prefer areas where the water is warmest. The deeper holes in the canal may also hold many reds. Dead shrimp will catch a mess of small reds, but use cut mullet or crab if it is you are after big ones. I have found squid an effective alternative. It has the right smell and its almost luminescent color adds visual appeal in dark water.

Something to keep in mind is that even small flows from a single drainpipe can draw fish. They may not hold massive schools of fish for long periods, but even a slight change in water temperature can make a big difference in cold weather. It is very important to look for the little things in these spots, since very often that is all it takes to attract game fish. One of the outfall canals I fish does not even pump hot water anymore, but the fish still congregate there. Old timers in the area say the fish in the area are "programmed" to go there. If that is true, then Mother Nature must program bull redfish to hit the jetties during winter. I grew up believing they only came nearshore during the fall, but found out there are plenty for anglers to find during winter at the jetties.

The largest concentrations of redfish seem to be at the deep holes at the southern tip of the Gulf side of jetties. If for some reason the deeper holes are inaccessible, you should back off and look for dips in the rocks. These dips indicate deep holes, and that is where the redfish will be. Another sign is vegetation growing on the bottom of the rocks. These areas hold lots of small crab, which makes excellent redfish bait. Shrimp is good, too. The advantage of using shrimp is that it is readily available, whereas crab can be tough to come by. Shrimp has one serious drawback though. Everything in the ocean eats it, so sometimes a redfish does not get a chance to get the bait.

I generally put out several lines with a slip egg weight and swivel, finished off with a wide gapped hook. This simple set up is ideal for catching reds, but knowing when to set the hook is another issue entirely. For some reason, bull redfish like to peck on bait during winter. Other times of year, they slam whatever you throw at them with great fury, but during winter, they peck for a while and then take off. The best setup is to place the rod in a holder and turn on the reel clicker. When the clicker starts to sound, turn it off and reel in the slack. When it feels like your rod is water bound, set the hook.

A few years ago, a letter from a reader led me to a spot at the Sabine

Lisa Moore caught her first ever bull redfish while fishing in the middle of a thunderstorm at Meacom's Pier.

Jetties where slot-size redfish were gathered around large concentrations of menhaden and suspended in 25 feet of water. By running my fish-finder, it did not take long to find the shad. There were millions of them as the entire middle section of the screen looked like a solid piece of structure. I put on a live menhaden, slowly lowered it to the desired depth, and immediately got a strike.

During winter redfish tend to stick around warm-water discharges and in deep areas. This angler caught this particular specimen on Sabine Lake.

My rod bent in half and I was battling a nice redfish. After landing that fish, I quickly hooked up with another and ended up catching 20 between 23 and 36 inches. Some might say I was a lunatic for being on the water that day—the air temperature was in the mid 30s and the wind chill had to be in the upper teens. Truly understanding jetties is crucial to being able to catch fish there. They might look like a simple pile of useless rocks, but there is more to it than that.

To start with, the rocks are three times wider at the bottom than they are at the surface, which means you have more structure than meets the eye. The real structure is below the surface—pockets in the rocks and deep holes that create eddies and strong currents.

It is crucial to move until you find fish. During winter months, I never give one spot more than 20 minutes if I have not caught a sheepshead, redfish, redfish, or redfish. Fish are gregarious, especially during winter and the angler who finds one fish should find much more where that one came from.

When fishing jetties from a boat, anchoring technique is a major issue. Use lots of rope. About 125 feet should be enough. Between the rope and anchor there should be at least five feet of heavy chain. This helps keep the anchor on the bottom. Never shut off the engine while anchoring. You could easily drift into the rocks and cause severe damage to your boat and possibly yourself. Keep the boat up-current from the intended fishing hole and then drop the anchor. I have been using an anchor called the Mighty-Mite and have found it the ultimate jetty anchor. It has specially designed teeth that provide a steady grip but still dislodge from just about any rocky crevice with relative ease.

Chapter Three

Reds on Top are Tops

Redfish are to topwater plugs what A-10 Warthogs are to Iraqi tanks: destruction. Reds do not just "hit" a plug, they strike it with such great force you would think they have some personal beef with it. Trout "smack" or "slurp" topwaters, whereas reds pounce like a cougar on an unwary whitetail. I have always said that if anglers consider what trout do a "blowup," they should call a topwater redfish strike "nuclear holocaust."

Despite the dramatics, most anglers' experiences with reds on topwaters come while pursuing speckled trout. The scenario usually goes something like this: An eager angler walks a Top Dog along a promising piece of shoreline. It is where his friend caught a 10-pounder last week and he hopes its siblings are still in the area. As his mind focuses on walking the dog just right, a mighty explosion rocks the surface. The rod doubles over and the fisherman's heart races as his dreams of catching a double-digit trout seem within reach. Then he notices his quarry is not silver but bronze, and then comes the final blow when a telltale spotted tail breaks the water. Then comes a slew of profanity-laden tirades.

"It's just a blanking redfish!"

"I blanking hate redfish!"

"If I catch another blanking redfish I'm going to scream!"

For hardcore trout fanatics, these are trying times. But for those of us who hold reds in high regard, they are times of pure joy.

Accidental encounters are common, but it is possible to target redfish with topwater lures. It just takes a little focus, willingness to try something different, and a heart strong enough to withstand intense excitement. The first thing to consider is where to fish. This might seem obvious, but the fact is some anglers just go to areas frequented by reds and assume they will have luck with topwaters. That is not the case.

The key to catching reds on topwaters is to be able to see them or at least locate signs of their feeding. Deep oyster reefs, for example, hold plenty of reds, but hooking one on a topwater there is not going to happen, at least not with any frequency.

I cut my teeth pursuing topwater reds in shallow marshes along the Upper Texas Coast, where I threw directly to the fish I wanted to catch. I could selectively target a big 30-inch brute or a barely legal sized 20-incher for the frying pan. It was truly a beautiful thing. My first successful outing was in a place called the "Twin Lakes" in Bridge City. Now part of the Lower Neches Wildlife Management Area, it serves as an intake reservoir for an Entergy Power Plant. The spot we scored on was a shallow flat that bordered two small islands in the marsh. The water in this spot was always super clear, so finding reds there was not a difficult task. The hardest part was not spooking them, so my father and I devised a shrewd game plan. We would come from the backside of the island by boat, anchor, and then walk across the island and fish from the bank. I have used this technique in other places, such as East Galveston Bay and Lake Calcasieu, where I found similar shallow, clear flats that held redfish.

Another good location for topwater reds is along shorelines in 2 to 3 feet of water. This sometimes requires a little closer observation than on the super

Chugging-style topwater plugs are tops for big redfish.

shallow flats because the reds are not always visible. A telltale sign of redfish in these spots is mud boils spawned by the fish foraging around for crabs. Capt. Guy Schultz, who operates on Galveston Bay, is an Apache helicopter pilot for the Army reserve. He said while flying over that bay system he has seen trails of mud boils stretching for miles. From high up, these are easy to locate, but on the water they are not so easy to find.

If you are in a shallow area that you know reds school in, simply look for changes in water clarity. Fish the edges of the clear and murky and there is a good chance you will find redfish. Sometimes big schools of reds are responsible for screwing up water quality, so do not be afraid to give these spots a try.

An overlooked but excellent spot to catch reds on topwaters is along the weir systems that are common in Louisiana, and becoming more common in Texas. Reds in these locations feed on the shrimp, crab, and other creatures that dwell near the top of the weir, and so they feed close to the surface. It is not unusual to see the reds surface feeding in these areas. Sub-surface lures are more popular for fishing these spots, but topwaters get the job done and then some.

I have caught Louisiana limits (five fish) of big reds on topwaters in the Cameron Prairie National Wildlife Refuge on the eastern side of Lake Calcasieu, and at Burton's Ditch, just five minutes from my home on the Louisiana side of the Sabine River.

Dan Olfatz of Alabama told me he catches reds on topwaters during high tides in tidal pools along the beaches in Alabama and Florida. He said the reds gather in the pools to feed on crab and will hit virtually anything you throw at them. My only experience catching reds on topwaters in the surf was the time I spotted some feeding along the rocks at Constance Beach in southwest Louisiana. I simply cast parallel to the rocks and yanked out redfish after redfish.

Something I learned early on was that redfish would only hit a lure put in front of them or directly to their side. They would never detect splashing behind them and turn around to investigate.

Later on, Ed Holder taught me about the red's "cone of vision." He said you have a 180-degree area from one eye, across the nose, and to the other eye to throw in and stay in the fish's sight. He said the best spot to cast is a few feet right in front of the red. They like to make a direct attack.

Many anglers, particularly on the Lower Texas Coast, talk about sight-casting to "tailing" redfish. What they mean is the reds are feeding in the shallows and their tails are sticking out of the water. In my region, we rarely saw "tailing" reds, but lots of "finning" ones. In other words, their backs and dorsal fin would stick out of the water. Finding "tailing" reds is quite exciting, however, and can give the angler a good sense of where to cast. If the tail is facing one way, then the head will be in the opposite direction. This might seem obvious, but in the excitement of the moment, such things are sometimes hard to remember. While wade-fishing in the Chandeleur Islands back in the summer of 2000, I came across a bunch of reds tailing. I was so excited at what I had found that I cast directly past their tails. While walking my Top Dog toward the fish, I realized the tail was facing me and their head was going the other direction. That one still embarrasses me.

Gearing up for topwater redfishing requires no great preparation, but there are a few things to consider for optimum angling. A medium-heavy casting rod is ideal, and I prefer them a little on the heavy side. Reds are not particularly difficult to hook, but I make long casts with surface plugs, so I prefer a rod with backbone to help get a good hookset. After decades of fishing on the Gulf Coast, I am still amazed that a fish could hit a topwater plug armed

Jason Carter throws a topwater for reds along a shoreline. Topwaters are not only fun to use but highly effective for catching reds in the shallows. Note the egret in the background. Egrets are always an indicator for the presence of baitfish.

with three treble hooks and not get stuck. To maximize hookset on reds, I have experimented with braided and fusion line (super line) and have had mixed results. The hookset advantage over monofilament is undeniable since super lines feature no-stretch properties. The problem comes with fighting the fish close to the boat. I have had several big reds make sudden, jerky runs right at the boat and break off. This is not a problem with monofilament.

My favorite monofilament is Berkley Big Game, but Stren Sensor is also good, along with Triple Fish and Excalibur. Nowadays, it is hard to go wrong with monofilament. If you choose to use braid for redfish, back off the drag a little once the fish gets close to the boat. If the fish starts to get away from you, it will be easy to readjust.

As far as plugs go, reds are not very fussy. In the lure chapter, I list a variety of topwaters and matching colors that I have field tested and found effective. The lure we used on my early outings in the "Twin Lakes" was the Jumpin' Minnow in bone color. If walked quickly, the reds would follow the plug, but rarely strike. When we slowed the presentation, watch out; a strike was inevitable.

My personal favorite topwaters for reds are walkers like the Top Dog, She Dog, Super Spook, and others. Some anglers call the Jumpin' Minnow a walker, but I do not really see it that way. They do walk, not in the same way as a Ghost or Top Dog. I especially like the Skitter Walk because it is by far the easiest to walk of any topwater I have ever fished—and I mean all of them. I discovered the lure while fishing in the Chandeleur Islands with Keith Warren and could not believe how simple it was to walk. That made it easy to fish and easy on my wrist after a hard day of fishing.

Despite what some anglers might tell you, there is no magic to walking a lure for reds other than the lure should twitch back and forth in a fluid motion. On the other hand, chuggers are effective and are great for making lots of noise and erratic motion. I have found chuggers like the Rattlin' Chug Bug and Pop-R great for catching reds in murkier water. I fish them more aggressively and drive

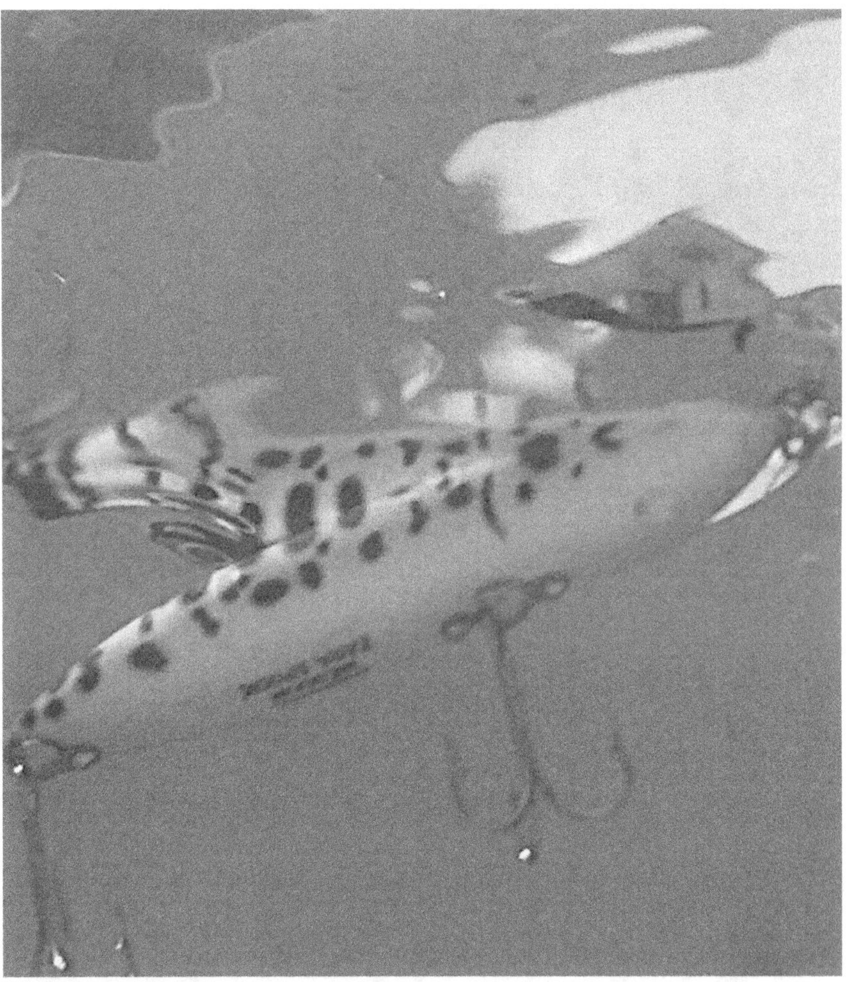

Watching a redfish take a topwater in the shallows makes for heart-pounding excitement.

my friends crazy with all of the noise I make. When the water is murky, I believe we need to give the fish all of the indicators we can so they can find and hit our plugs. "Wild" Bill Skinner of Bass-N-Mexico sold me on this when he came to Texas to seek redfish with me. The water was off-colored so he went to his tackle box and broke out some chuggers he designed himself. He caught plenty of reds and got me to rethink the use of chuggers for the species.

Speaking of hitting our plugs, it really is a miracle that redfish can hit anything on the surface. God designed them to feed on bottom-dwelling crustaceans, so they have to turn over or at least on their side to hit a topwater. Perhaps the reason they hit plugs with such gusto is they figure if they are going through the trouble of turning over to hit the thing, they might as well destroy it. That is why I love catching reds on topwaters so much. Outside of gator wrestling, it is the most intense thing going in Texas and Louisiana bay systems—and it's a tad bit safer. Well, it is for the angler. The plugs themselves do not have much of a life expectancy.

Chapter Four

Redfish School

I could not believe my eyes.

An acre-wide patch of water southwest of the Galveston Jetties churned and boiled with great fury. For a moment it seemed as if a nuclear submarine was surfacing, concern for national security eased when I saw mullet scurrying in the bronze-tinged mass of water, trying to avoid violent death by a massive school of bull redfish—and I do mean massive. My jaw dropped and heart pounded at what I was witnessing. This was an angler's dream and I was experiencing it in vivid, living color.

Realizing that schooling reds do not stay on the surface for long, I grabbed a rod rigged with a huge chugging topwater plug and fired it toward the fracas. Before I could pop the lure, a monster red hammered it and shot out of the water like a bronze rocket. Redfish rarely go airborne, but when they do it is a remarkable sight. The battle took more than 15 minutes, and by that time, the school disappeared. I was elated, though, as 39 inches of measuring tape stretched from the red's nose to its tail. I knew there were bigger redfish in the school, but having caught a 39-incher on a topwater plug was a more than adequate consolation prize.

Beginning in mid-summer and lasting through the first couple of strong cold fronts in the fall, encounters like this are accessible to coastal anglers from Pensacola, Fla. to Port Mansfield, TX. Redfish begin to school *en masse* during calm, slick days in late June. Most anglers never find them because they are running back to the boat ramp when the feeding action begins. For some unknown reason, reds like to feed during the middle of the day when the temperatures soar and the bays are calm. Locating these fish requires glassing the bay and looking for water boiling and more subtle signs, like mysterious wakes and muddy patches surrounded by clear water. The key to successfully fishing these schools is to approach quietly. If you run up close and then throw over your trolling motor, you can forget it. These reds, despite their voracious nature, are very spooky. It is best to run up to them slowly, drop the trolling motor a hundred yards away, and ease in, or simply drift through them. I usually drift once I get close because even a trolling motor can put them down.

The beautiful thing about these reds is they will hit virtually anything. Live shrimp, croaker, mullet, spoons, lipless crankbaits, and soft plastics work just fine.

Sometimes, however, they are not so easy to locate and catch. Long time guide Capt. Skip James said school reds sometimes feed the outside edges of speckled trout schools instead of on the surface. During mid-summer, if you pick up a couple of reds in a school of trout, there are probably a bunch more lurking in the area.

"For a guy who's looking to bag some big reds and maybe has already caught his trout or would rather try something different, look to the outside of trout schools," James said. "Game fish feed in four distinct phases: packing, corralling, ambush, and mop-up. Packing involves the fish coming together to terrorize the baitfish population. This usually happens early on." It's during the next phase, corralling, that we start to notice some action, like nervous

Schooling redfish cause commotion unlike any other inland species.

menhaden, scurrying shrimp and jumping ladyfish. During the ambush period, the feeding reaches a feverish frenzy, as the fish turn from passive to highly aggressive. This is the phase that the birds work, and it is when you want to have your bait in the water.

"To catch schooling reds, I recommend a lipless crankbait or a big heavy spoon. Use something that you can chunk out there and reach the fish with, and that can get down toward the bottom fast. Additionally, have a few extra guns ready to shoot with. If you catch the fish on the feed, do not bother to unhook your fish if it is a legal one. Just lay it down for a second and fire another shot. It's important to maximize your time during the feeding frenzy."

James said that when targeting reds, it is crucial to avoid the small trout. He recommends backing off of a school if you catch a couple of small trout.

They will get your bait before the reds do, so leave them be: "If I go in and catch a couple of little trout right off of the bat, I circle where I think the school is and try to find the reds. Often, they will be on the outer edges of the trout, but you may have to search a little to find them."

The final stage of a feeding phase is mop-up. This occurs after the main feeding is over and the fish seemingly get lockjaw. This is a great time to move into an area where trout have been schooling to locate reds. More often than not, they will move in on the remnants of a baitfish school and start biting when the trout leave.

"When the main bite is over, I will switch over from a lipless crankbait or spoon to a soft plastic swimbait rigged on a jighead and bounce it along the

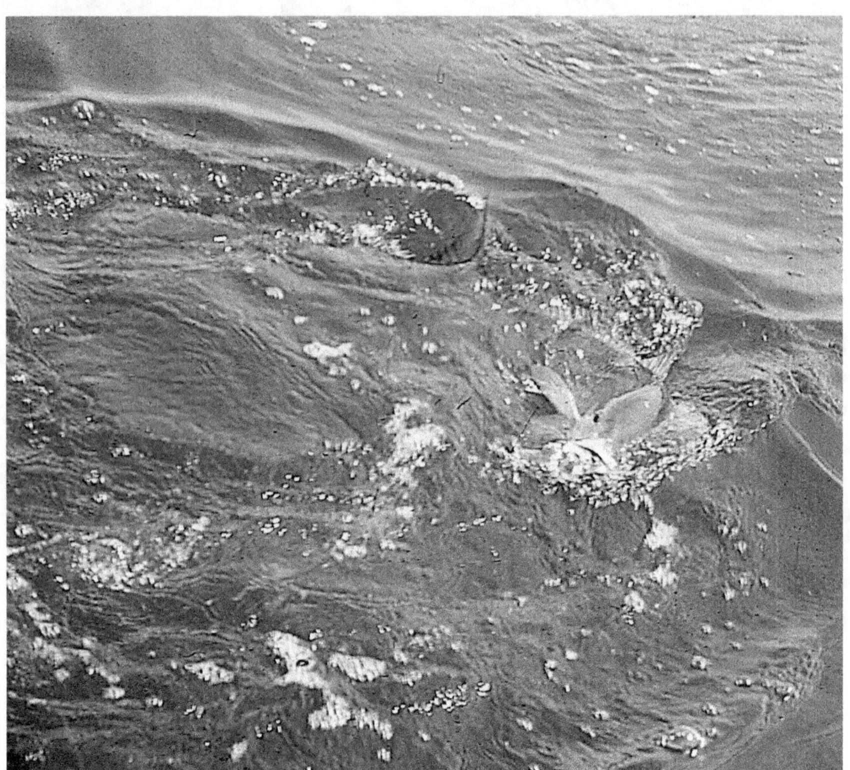

Churning and boiling water laced with a slight of bronze or like in this case a spotted tail sticking out of the water is a sure sign redfish are schooling in an area.

bottom, trying to rattle any roving reds attention. Glow and chartreuse are the best colors," James said.

James believes a common mistake is to leave an area during the mop-up period. The best bet is to set the trolling motor on low and cruise the perimeter, making 45-degree fan casts so that you can cover every angle. Think of redfish as scavengers waiting to attack the remnants of the trout's prey. As summer wears on, action picks up in the nearshore Gulf of Mexico. Capt. Jim Leavelle said anglers can find monstrous schools of redfish from a few hundred yards from the surf on out to a couple of miles: "It's one of the most beautiful things you will ever encounter on the Texas coast. We have captured this phenomenon on video and people are always amazed at what they see." These schooling reds will do one of two things: totally ignore your efforts or hit just about anything thrown at them. "Sometimes these reds can be spooky, so you have to be careful in approaching them," Leavelle said.

He is right. They may seem fearless as they madly thrash the water's surface, but they are actually a very cautious fish. In fact, I have found them to be twice as cautious as the smaller reds in the bay, and that may be an understatement. Follow the protocol for the schools in the bay, but remember this: If they disappear, approach the area where you last saw them and begin drifting. Sometimes they will follow the current to catch up with whatever they have been feeding on, so drifting is a good way to find them without making noise. Starting up the big motor is a no-no.

I have caught these reds on topwaters, lipless crankbaits, and spoons, but by far the all-around best bait is a live croaker. I have never thrown a croaker into one of these schools that did not get gobbled up in short order. Big, bull redfish cannot resist live croaker, especially when they are in a feeding frenzy. The chances of catching them on lures is about 30 percent in my estimation, while using live croaker makes it virtually a done deal.

Something I noticed during one of my early encounters with Gulf schooling reds is the lack of gulls around them. The school that brought this to my attention was a few miles off the beach with no birds working, while just a couple of miles north, schools of small speckled trout drew in plenty of bird action. This has spawned debate among anglers who see it. One school of thought is the reds are targeting the Gulf menhaden. Still other anglers have said the reds are chasing large mullet and the gulls would rather pick off small shad and shrimp kicked up by the trout instead of gulping down a big baitfish. That was my assumption since I could see pods of mullet around the school, but the plot thickened when I cleaned a trio of these Texas slot-sized reds. (Most of these schooling reds are over the legal size limit and I release them to fight another day.) Two of them had empty stomachs while the other was stuffed with cutlass fish. These fish were all caught around 11 a.m. and it could be they had not fed since the previous day. All of the visible schooling action was during the mid-day slick offs. Empty stomachs could indicate these reds might be feeding on whatever they can kill for a few hours and not feed until around the same time the next day. The ones we caught might have just started feeding.

I would like to learn more about this to see if there is a discernible pattern to the behavior besides feeding during the mid-day period. The more I learn about them, the more I can catch. Moving on to fall, anglers can find less mysterious schools of reds that come out of the marshes on the Gulf Coast. These fish are easy to find and catch. Besides the splishing, splashing, and gulping sounds of feeding predatory fish, there are other obvious visual indicators—the shallow water they inhabit often takes on a bronze tint.

Jack's Pocket in Trinity Bay is routinely one of the best spots to seek schooling reds in the fall; it may be the best spot on the entire Texas coast. The easiest way to find these frenzy-feeding schools is by locating diving gulls picking off the nervous baitfish pushed to the surface. Nevertheless, do not rely solely on birds to find the fish. On one trip to Jack's Pocket, my partner and I fished successfully for quite a while without a single bird in view. Look for mud trails in the water, which often indicate redfish feeding.

Anglers typically throw spoons or soft plastic lures for these reds. I have used 12-pound test and a 3/8- to 1/2-ounce jighead to get past the small trout that often hang around the reds. The little specks feed on top as the reds are roving around the bottom. As Skip James recommended, fish down low to get the biggest and best fish.

Remember to drift over these schools rather than to fish them with a trolling motor. Once, a man fishing a school nearby me using his trolling motor only caught a few fish, while we had all the action we could handle. My friends and I watched him, and he was pursuing the fish too aggressively. You can catch fish that way, but I believe it is possible to catch far more the way we did it. These big schools can provide the kind of action few coastal anglers get to experience, so pay attention to the details.

As observed earlier, I have been fortunate enough to encounter red schools on many occasions and have made a list of words that accurately describe this kind of fishing: exciting, fantastic, cool, phenomenal, fun.

You have to love that.

I know I do.

Chapter Five

Natural Bait:

Ain't nothing like the real thing, baby

Nothing catches more redfish than natural bait. The vast majority of redfish landed along the Gulf and Atlantic coasts are caught on one of the following types of live bait, but it is not a one size fits all category here. Some of these baits are good for particular times of year and locations and are best fished on specific types of hooks and rigs. Pay special attention to detail even with natural bait and you will catch more and bigger redfish.

BLUE CRAB

Blue crab is the best overall redfish bait there is. Nature designed reds to feed on crab, outfitting them with a downward pointing mouth, which is highly effective for preying on bottom-dwelling crustaceans. Anglers typically pull the shell off the crab, split the body down the middle, and hook it through the carapace. (The carapace is the back leg that looks like a paddle.) When fishing for bull reds, most anglers prefer using the whole crab, once again, with the top popped off.

Live crab are also effective for reds, especially when fished around near-

God designed redfish to eat crabs. The author believes he is too, but he is not proficient enough to catch them with his mouth yet.

shore oil and gas platforms in the Gulf of Mexico. Hook them through the carapace and remove the claws for safer handling. A few years ago, I met a man who used soft shell crab for bull redfish during the fall run. While I am sure it works, I consider that a crime against humanity. Soft shell crab is my all-time favorite seafood and I cannot fathom using it for bait when I could put it in the frying pan and have an awesome meal. Catching redfish is great, but there is a point where I draw the line.

CROAKER

If I go out to specifically catch big reds, I always bring live croaker along. I have found it incredibly effective for drawing the strike of oversized reds in particular. I first discovered this while fishing at the Sabine Jetties after having sheepshead pick away the crab I was using. On my small rod, I caught an 8-inch croaker, hooked it through the lips, and tossed it out with one of my big rods. A few minutes later, it doubled over, and I was battling a 42-inch bull red. During the course of day, I caught nearly a dozen reds on live croaker, all of them oversized.

Croaker may be a better bait than blue crab for redfish, especially the big redfish.

Back in 1999, fishing travel agent "Wild" Bill Skinner came over from New Mexico to catch bull redfish. We went out to the Sabine Jetties and fished with light action spinning rods to catch croaker for bait. Skinner caught the first one, which was a foot long and started to cut it in half for bait. He looked at me as if I were crazy when I told him we would use it whole and alive. I quickly snatched up the croaker, put it on a wide-gapped hook and threw it overboard. Remember, this croaker was a foot long. A few minutes later, Skinner was battling a monstrous redfish that measured 43 inches. This story illustrates my point about live bait, particularly croaker for redfish: the bigger the bait, the bigger the fish.

Hook croaker through the mouth or tail for best action.

SHRIMP

Live shrimp are great redfish bait. They stay lively in livewells and active on a hook, plus they are a top prey item for reds during fall. The only drawback

Live shrimp can tempt just about any gamefish, including reds.

to shrimp is that virtually everything in the bay eats them, making them difficult to keep on the hook for long in redfish territory. Frozen shrimp is the most accessible bait around and is effective for redfish.

MULLET

Mullet is a popular redfish bait that is usually fished dead and cut. It is popular with surf fishermen targeting bull reds since mullet are easy to catch with cast nets. Live mullet is also good, and, like croaker, the rule is to use big bait to catch big fish. If you are targeting reds within the Texas slot limit, use smaller mullet. If you want a beast, do not be afraid to use mullet big enough to put in the frying pan.

MENHADEN

Menhaden, also known as pogies or shad, are another good choice. Moreover, like most redfish baits, they are effective both alive and dead. During late summer and fall, live menhaden fished under a popping cork on the main body of a bay is a killer method, especially when using an Alameda Rattler or a similar rattling cork rig. The ideal size is 3 to 4 inches long.

Keeping these delicate fish alive is a difficult task that I have only been able to do by using pure oxygen or an expensive recycling aeration system. They die quickly in hot weather.

A new trend among coastal anglers is fishing with "cold shad." This technique involves catching them by cast net and immediately putting them on a layer of ice and then covering them with another layer. Make sure to drain as much water out as possible to keep the shad fresh. Fish them just as you would the live version.

MUD MINNOW (GULF KILLIFISH, COCAHOE)

Mud minnows are underrated redfish bait. As detailed in my book, *Texas Trout Tactics*, several years ago while flounder fishing, I decided to use some left-over mud minnows for speckled trout, and it worked. What I did not mention

Redfish on reefs regularly encounter mud minnows, mullet and other small fish and the author has found of those three mud minnows are the best in getting them to strike on the reefs.

in that book is that we also caught many redfish that day.

While drifting a large oyster reef, my father and I fished with live mud minnows under popping corks. We caught a two-man limit of redfish on a reef that was 12 feet deep. We rigged our minnows to suspend about halfway down.

The main advantage to using mud minnows is they are a hardy fish that anglers can hook several ways: through both lips, behind the dorsal (top) fin, or through the body near the tail.

SAND TROUT

Sometimes when jetty fishing, croaker can be difficult to find, but sand trout are easy to catch. I have had good luck using both cut and live sand trout for reds. Sand trout stay on the hook well, too, but it is very appealing to sharks and stingrays. That does not bother me a bit, but for some anglers it is a little unnerving.

FIDDLER CRAB

These tiny crabs are hard to catch, but make excellent redfish bait, especially when fished in shallow salt marshes where they are common. Give them a chance if you cannot catch anything else.

PIGGY PERCH, PINFISH

These baitfishes are far more effective for catching speckled trout than redfish, but they do work from time to time. My advice would be to use them only as a last resort.

CRAWFISH

Redfish stocked in freshwater areas feed heavily on crawfish, and although it may seem a bit unorthodox, it works well in coastal marshes as well. Hook the crawfish through the tail so it stays alive.

CATCHING BAIT

A cast net is an indispensable tool for anglers serious about catching bait for redfish. I have been throwing a cast net since I was eight years old, and have

Cast nets are an indispensable tool for live bait fishermen.

always found it lots of fun. To this day, I take pride in catching my own bait.

Cast nets are great for catching mullet, menhaden, and shrimp, and can save thousands of dollars over a lifetime of fishing. If you are on a budget, learn to use a cast net because buying bait from a marina is expensive.

A tip for anglers new to using cast nets is to not use one that is too big. There is no shame in using a 6-foot net while others around you are using 12- and 14-footers. It does you no good to use a huge net if you cannot throw it correctly. Accuracy in casting can make up for width of a net.

Cast nets cannot catch all baitfishes effectively, and crab are a prime example. The best way to get crab is to buy a crab trap and set it out the night before you go fishing. You can purchase traps for about $30 at commercial fishing supply stores. They are an invaluable tool for anglers serious about using crab.

Mud minnows are caught mostly in traps, which sell for about half of what a good crab trap costs. Mud minnow traps can be set along shallow ditches in the marsh or near the bay and are extremely efficient. Perch traps, which are available at commercial fishing outlets and some bait shops, are good for catching piggy perch, pinfish, and croaker.

I have found it is best to use rod and reel to catch croaker. I like to use (the really big ones). I usually use croaker while jetty fishing, so I bring along a light action-spinning rod rigged with a double leader and baited with dead shrimp. If there are croaker in the area, it does not take long to find them, then when I put the croaker on as bait, it does not take redfish long to find *them*.

Sand trout, as noted earlier, are a good substitute for croaker and anglers can catch them the same way. The only difference is I catch larger sand trout on cut bait rather than shrimp. I recommend a treble hook for sand trout, but cut bait is a magnet for hardheads and there is nothing more annoying than having to remove a treble hook from these dangerous-to-handle fish.

KEEPING BAIT ALIVE

The secret to using live bait is simple: keep it alive. Well, the concept may be simple, but actually keeping some baitfishes breathing can be a challenge.

For bank fishermen, a large Styrofoam ice chest will do a good job keeping most baitfishes kicking. Styrofoam breathes and if the water is changed periodically, most bait will do well.

For anglers in boats, a recirculating livewell is the ideal setup. By exchanging water frequently, anglers can achieve low bait mortality in many situations. A great aid to keeping bait alive is chemical additives produced by Sure-Life Laboratories. They have chemicals out called Pogy-Saver, Croaker-Saver, Shrimp-Saver, and stuff designed especially for mullet and many other baitfishes. A couple of spoonfuls of this stuff will help eliminate ammonia in the water, a byproduct produced naturally by the baitfishes themselves which kills

Wanna keep bait alive? If so, David Kinser shows how he does it with an oxygen bottle. Putting pure oxygen into the water is essential to keeping baitfish kicking.

accumulates and kills them.

Unbelievably, some anglers use sawdust to keep shrimp alive. Back in the 1970's and early 1980's, some bait camps sold live shrimp in sawdust. Some, particularly in Florida, still carry on this tradition. Sawdust holds in moisture and actually keeps the shrimp alive longer than just sitting in a regular bait bucket. The strange thing is that it is very important not to dampen the sawdust too much. It will kill the shrimp.

A similar technique involves an ordinary towel. Bring along a towel and wet it with the water the shrimp came from. Then fold the towel in half and place it in your cooler. After that, lift the top layer of the towel and put the shrimp all over the towel in a single layer. Then fold it back down so it covers the shrimp.

This will cause the shrimp to look dead, but they are really in a state of suspended animation and can live for up to 24 hours. As soon as you hook the shrimp and put it in the water, it will come alive. If you are dead set on keeping bait alive you need to use pure, dissolved oxygen. I have been a proponent of David Kinser's Oxygen Edge system for years. It is the best investment I have ever made for live bait fishing. Having had an Oxygen Edge Unit since early

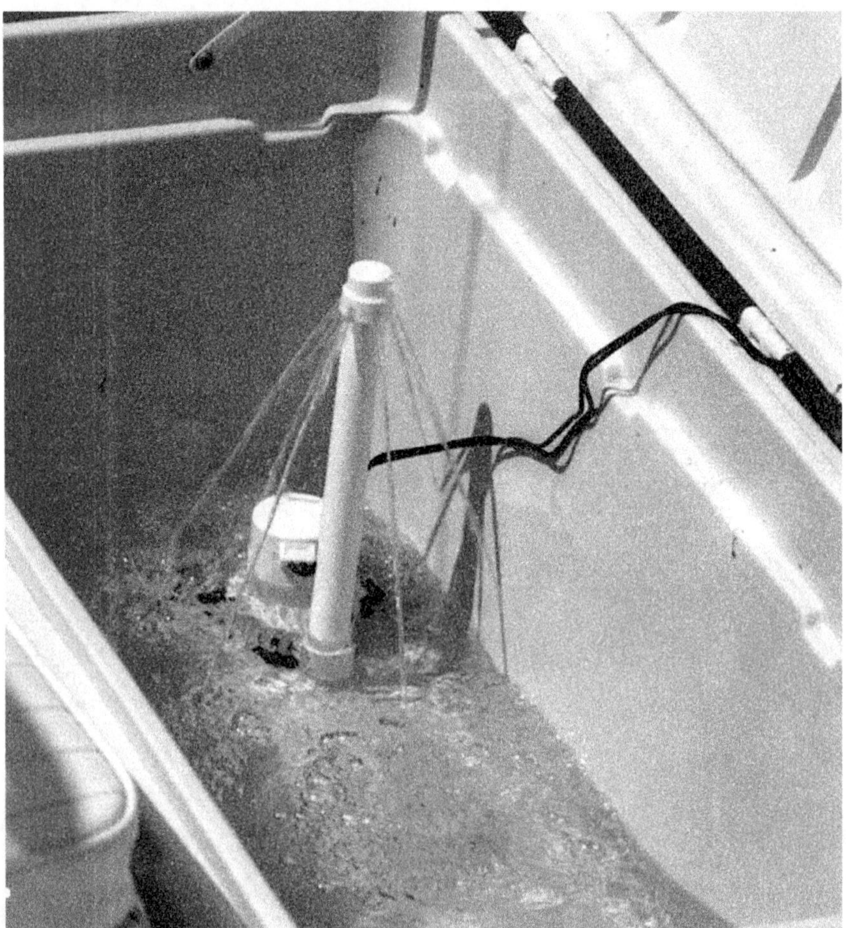

Aerators are the standard way of caring for baitfish.

1998, I can attest to its absolute effectiveness. Speaking very conservatively, it has reduced live bait mortality in my live well by 80 percent.

Instead of relying on standard aeration to keep bait or tournament fish alive, Kinser's system involves super-charging the water with pure oxygen.

"Standard aeration systems draw from the air, which is composed of 21 percent oxygen." Kinser said. "Factor in that many units only achieve 65 to 80 percent efficiency, and it becomes obvious what happens when water temperatures start to heat up. The fish start to die because they are not getting enough oxygen."

Another advantage of using the Oxygen Edge is that it keeps baitfish "super-charged." The oxygen keeps their metabolism so high that they are very frisky and more likely to attract a response from a game fish.

According to the Bait Care Company, when shad are held in bait buckets, they are usually very crowded. This results in physical abrasion, poisonous ammonia build-up, and short-lived bait. They say to keep shad healthy, add Shad Protector as soon as the fish go in the bucket. Keep the bait bucket out of the sun. Cooler water holds more oxygen and makes it easier for the fish to breathe. If the water in the bait bucket looks dirty, change half of the water and add another dose of Shad Protector. Repeat this procedure throughout the day as necessary. When keeping shad in a bucket for an extended time, a battery-powered aerator is recommended to maintain an adequate oxygen level.

Chapter Six

The Artificial Approach

Some of the first lures designed specifically for saltwater were produced to target redfish. Back in the 1950's, anglers began throwing gold spoons at reds on the coast and found the fish responded favorably to these simple chunks of metal. A few years later, a few soft plastic lures designed for reds hit the market, with early models closely resembling crude bass worms.

When I was a kid, we rarely used lures for redfish, but the store we stopped at before going fishing had a small lure rack stocked with a locally made "redfish lure," which was a 6-inch, pink plastic worm with a white jighead and another hook rigged toward the tail. This thing fascinated me, so one day Dad bought me one to try. I never caught a red on it, but I sure had fun fishing with it.

Nowadays, there are hundreds of lures made for redfish and they are all fun to fish. There is just something about a red hitting a lure that makes me want to go fishing.

Enough with the remembrances, let' look at some good redfish lures.

LURE: Johnson Spoon

BEST SEASON(s): Year-round

COLOR: Gold or Bronze

APPLICATION/LOCATION: Throw to areas where reds are visibly attacking baitfishes, or work along drop-offs and in grassy areas. When reds are schooling, this a good lure to throw because you can get distance on it and not spook the fish.

TECHNIQUE: Chuck it out, reel it in with a varying retrieve. When fishing jetties or deep holes, chunk it out and let it flutter.

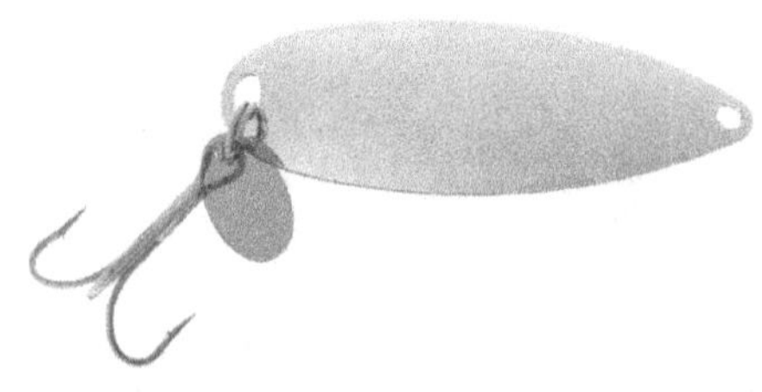

Johnson Spoon

TIPS: If you are serious about catching redfish, this is a must-have. There is no better basic redfish lure.

LURE: Gulp! Swimming Mullet

BEST SEASON(s): Year-round

COLOR: New Penny, smoke, pink

APPLICATION/LOCATION: This will literally work anywhere and anytime.

TECHNIQUE: My favorite way to fish this is under a loud popping cork. The combination of the scent of the Gulp! and the sound of the cork will draw in reds.

TIPS: Fish on a jighead that has grooves to screw into the Gulp! That will help keep it on there as hard-hitting reds do their best to take it off for eating purposes.

Gulp! Swimming Mullet

LURE: Bomber Saltwater Grade Super Pogy

BEST SEASON: Spring/Summer/Fall

COLOR: Chrome/blue, Bronze, white/red

APPLICATION/LOCATION: This one is perfect for picking out distant pieces of structure you don't want to approach too closely. You can cast it a long way and it is easy to work.

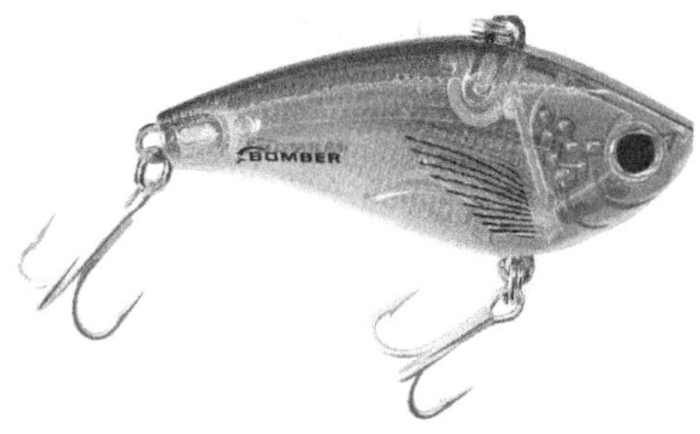

Bomber Saltwater Grade Super Pogy

TECHNIQUE: Throw it out, let it sink a few seconds and then rip it. Reel a few feet slowly and rip again. Repeat the process until you reach the boat.

TIPS: If you are fishing by deep rocks at a jetty, let it sink about five seconds and then start ripping. Many times the suspended reds will hit it on the fall.

LURE: DOA Shrimp

BEST SEASON(s): Summer, Fall

COLOR: Clear, glow, chartreuse, root beer

APPLICATION/LOCATION: Since it is weedless, this is a good lure to fish in the marsh during the high tides that often come in later summer and early fall.

TECHNIQUE: Throw around clumps of grass in marsh and in areas with heavy vegetation. Aim for specific areas and work over heavily.

TIPS: Do not be afraid to drag through heavy grass. The lure makers designed it for fishing in the grass.

DOA Shrimp

LURE: Sebile Splasher

COLOR: Various

BEST SEASON(s): Spring, Summer, Fall

APPLICATION/LOCATION: This lure is excellent for catching schooling reds in the late summer and fall.

TECHNIQUE: As the name implies, this lure is a "chugger." Use a quick twitch of the rod tip to make the dished-out face "chug" and throw spray.

TIPS: I caught my biggest ever topwater red on this lure sight-casting in Venice, La. The key pattern for me is to throw it out, let it sit a second, give it two pops and let it sit for 3-5 seconds. You will usually get hit just before you decide to pop again.

Sebile Splasher

LURE: Twister Tail

COLOR: White, Chartreuse, Glow

BEST SEASON(s): Year-round

APPLICATION/LOCATION: This lure is best fished on a 1/8- or 1/4-ounce jighead around the mouth of marsh points and along the shorelines of bay systems. This is not a good lure to fish in heavy current.

TECHNIQUE: Drag slowly across the bottom or moderately hop it up and down.

TIPS: There is another version of this lure called the Spin Top combo that has a slightly different jighead and a small teardrop-bladed spinner fitted on it. It is hard to find, but an excellent lure.

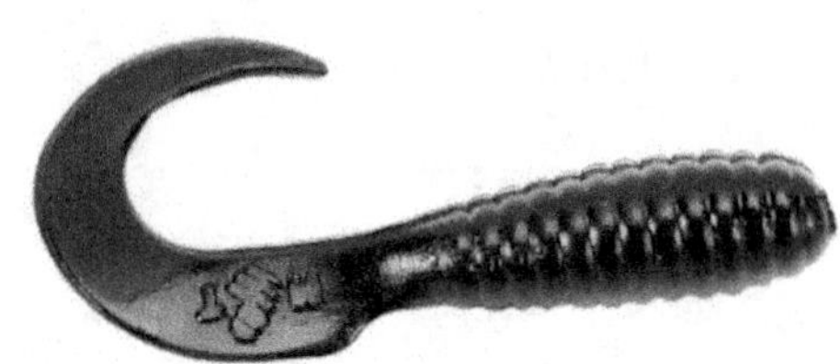

Twister Tail

LURE: MirrOlure Top Dog
COLOR: Bone, Black, Chartreuse.
BEST SEASON(s): Spring, Summer, Fall
APPLICATION/LOCATION: Fish this one anywhere you think a topwater explosion could happen.
TECHNIQUE: Walk the dog, plain and simple.
TIPS: The Top Dog is one of the most popular lures of all time, and for good reason. It is easy to walk, cast, and catch fish on. I like to use this with braided line. I find the lure walks better and the braided line increases my hook-to-land ratio.

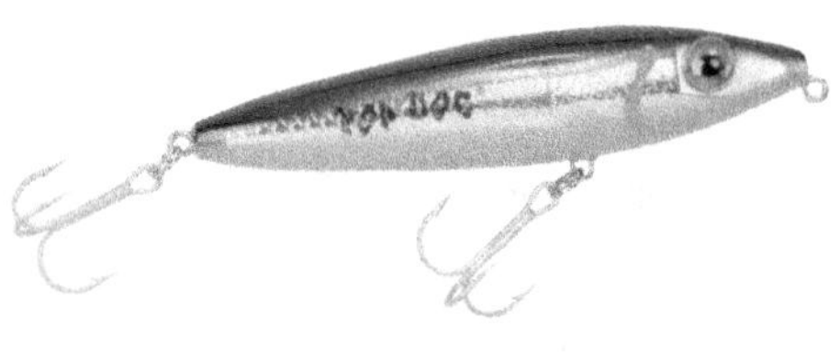
MirrOlure Top Dog

LURE: Norton Sand Eel
BEST SEASON(s): Spring
COLOR: Glow/Chartreuse, Pearl, Red Shad
APPLICATION/LOCATION: This lure is a fine imitator of the sand eel, which is a chief prey item of reds in the early spring. It can catch reds anywhere, but is best fished over oyster reefs.
TECHNIQUE: I have found this lure to be effective when fished on a 3/8-ounce jighead and bounced on the bottom.
TIPS: This lure, unlike the Sabine Snake, should not be fished with a fast retrieve. It moves quickly through the water on its own in areas of strong current.

Norton San Eel

LURE: Rat-L-Trap

BEST SEASON(s): Year-round

COLOR: Chrome and Black, Chrome and Blue

APPLICATION/LOCATION: Open bays, shorelines, cuts, and offshore around oil rigs

TECHNIQUE: Most anglers are familiar with ripping this lure through schools of reds or using it as a locater to work down shorelines and canals. A virtually unknown but highly effective method for the 'Trap involves letting it hit the bottom and slowly scooting it. This is killer during winter months when reds are more sluggish. Around oil rigs in the nearshore Gulf, throw it out, let flutter down around the platform legs, and reel up with a medium retrieve.

Rat-L-Trap

TIPS: Use a shock leader to lessen the chances of losing these expensive lures.

LURE: Skitter Walk

BEST SEASON(s): Spring, Summer, Fall

COLOR: Bone

APPLICATION/LOCATION: Like the Top Dog, fish this one anywhere you think a topwater explosion could happen.

TECHNIQUE: Walk the dog.

TIPS: When a red first hits this lure, do not set the hook hastily. Let the fish take some line then make a hookset.

Skitter Walk

LURE: Fat Free Shad

BEST SEASON(s): Summer, Fall

COLOR: Tennessee Shad Chrome

APPLICATION/LOCATION: Use this in ship channels to locate reds hanging in deep water, and at jetties.

TECHNIQUE: Rip this one through the water fast, or rip it fast in short bursts, let it suspend, and repeat.

TIPS: This lure was designed for bass, but it is great for redfish.

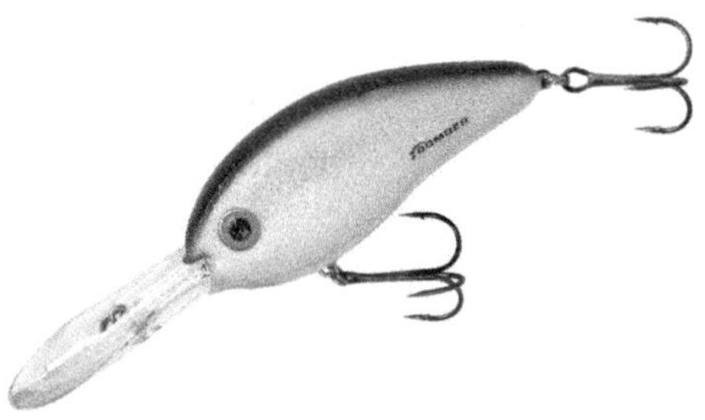

Fat Free Shad

LURE: H&H 1/2-ounce spinnerbait

BEST SEASON(s): Summer, fall

COLOR: White, Yellow, Chartreuse

APPLICATION/LOCATION: Yet another bass lure, this is a great one to fish in the marsh around grass lines and in the mouths of cuts.

TECHNIQUE: Spinners are easy to fish. Simply slow-roll it or use a fast retrieve. I usually start with a slow roll, then go to a fast retrieve if the fish do not respond.

TIPS: Do not feel goofy for using this on redfish; it works.

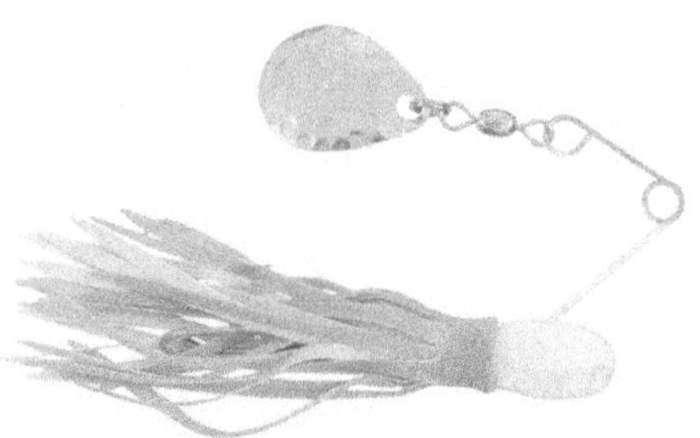

H&H 1/2-Ounce Spinnerbait

LURE: Sassy Shad

BEST SEASON(s): Spring, Summer, Fall

COLOR: Natural Shad, Pearl, Chartreuse

APPLICATION/LOCATION: In spring, use the smallest version of the lure to fish in eddies where small shad go to rest. During summer and fall, go to the big 5-inch to target reds feeding on larger menhaden.

Sassy Shad

TECHNIQUE: Drag the lure slowly across the bottom or hop it up and down.

TIPS: Be mindful of size for the different seasons. You have to "match the hatch," so to speak. The rule of thumb is small in spring and larger in summer and fall.

LURE: Arbogast Hula Popper

COLOR: Various

BEST SEASON(s): Spring, Summer, Fall

APPLICATION/LOCATION: This old bass fishing lure is excellent for catching schooling in late summer and fall. I first learned of its effectiveness when fishing the marshes of Venice, Louisiana, where it is a popular redfish bait.

Arbogast Hula Popper

TECHNIQUE: As the name implies, this lure is a "popper." Twitch the rod tip to make it pop and splash.

TIPS: If you get "followers" that will not strike, stop the lure, stick your rod tip beneath the surface, then reel in very fast. The lure will dive beneath the surface and wobble through the water, leaving a trail of bubbles. This can elicit a "reaction strike."

LURE: Shad Assassin

COLOR: Various

BEST SEASON(s): Winter, Early Spring

APPLICATION/LOCATION: This is a slow-sinking plastic that anglers sometimes use without a jighead during winter.

TECHNIQUE: Fish with a very slow retrieve.

TIPS: Try this lure fished "wacky style." Hook the lure in the center and let it sink without a weight. It works great for bass, and I have caught quite a few reds and trout that way.

Shad Assassin

LURE: Berkley Power Mullet

BEST SEASON(s): Summer, Fall

COLOR: Glow/Chartreuse, Purple/Yellow for murky conditions

APPLICATION/LOCATION: This is a good lure for fishing in river systems and marshes above bays, where reds are common.

TECHNIQUE: This is a good lure to use on a fish-finder (Carolina) rig, and it is good to bounce on the bottom.

TIPS: Bring a bunch. Reds tear up this one.

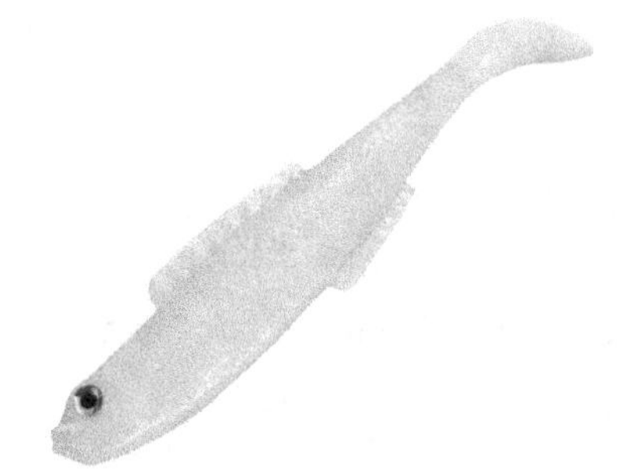

Berkley Power Mullet

MODIFYING LURES

Many anglers are no longer relying on lure manufacturers to produce specific colors, shapes, and actions in lures. Many of them are adapting to conditions in the waters they fish to come up with some unusual and productive modifications.

A reader sent a very interesting topwater modification to me. He links three Rattlin' Chug Bugs together with 80-pound Spiderwire. The first lure is a Big Bug, the second is the standard Chug Bug, and the third is a Baby Bug. He said it imitates a school of baitfish. He simply pops or chugs the lure instead of walking the dog with it. Judging from the digital picture he sent of some of the fish he caught using this modification, I may try it myself this year.

Soft plastic lures are easy to modify and coastal anglers often experiment with them. Colorite Bait Coloring System produced by the Colorite Bait Company (colorite@flash.net) out of Alvin, Texas, makes modifications easy. One of my favorite colors for topwater is anything with a red head and white body. Once I got the Colorite system, I translated this over to plastics by taking a white shrimp tail and dipping the first half-inch in a red tail dip. This stuff dries quickly and stays with the lure, which makes it practical to carry along on a fishing trip for last minute modifications.

A bass angler from Kentucky sent me one of the neatest modifications I have seen, and I believe could be productive for redfish. When fishing a Texas rig for bass, he rigs up two worms instead of one. He puts on a barrel swivel and then makes two one-foot leaders down to a worm hook and bullet weight, and then hooks on his worms. He claims this drives the bass crazy and has helped him to win several local fishing tournaments. I have considered using this for saltwater fishing with the Norton Sand Eel or Culprit Worm, both excellent lures for imitating the eels so common on Texas oyster reefs. I pour some of my own jigheads, so I have made jigheads with a double hook. I am going to fish the lures close together and see what happens. For anglers who do not have their own equipment for this, just use the Texas-rig method. It will produce

This rack of plugs has been battered, beaten and abused.

about the same action as a jighead, and it might be fun to tell your friends you smoked the reds on a Texas-rigged worm. They may never believe you, but it does not matter if you catch fish.

The simple addition of a popping cork can give a lure an entirely different life. While drift-fishing over heavy grass or structure, it might pay to fish a Rat-L-Trap under a popping cork, especially during winter months when the fish's metabolism is slow. The movement of the current should keep the action going, and by using a cork, it is possible to stay away from tangles. In addition, the popping of the cork gives it a unique action.

Call me crazy, call me strange, but these modifications work. Sometimes fish do not like to cooperate, so we have to influence them a little. I say, when it comes to catching reds, the motto should be "by all means necessary." That includes the weird stuff.

TIPS FROM THE PROS

The next time you go for redfish, consider these tips from the experts at Berkley.

1. A good angler hears and sees well and his or her mind instantly registers the impressions. If a redfish nails a baitfish on the surface behind you, your ears should convey the message. The trick is to train our senses to accept the commonplace sights and sounds in nature and seek out the unusual. Always be alert on the water.

2. Most anglers put life into a soft plastic lure by using the reel instead of the rod. That is entirely the wrong approach. Dragging a lure with the reel robs the lure of its built-in action. Instead, keep the rod tip high while using it to move the life-like piece of plastic. Lift the rod to move the lure, allow it to settle down to the bottom, and then reel in the excess slack.

4. One of the most deadly techniques for soft-plastic lures like jigs and

grubs is vertical jigging. One way to trigger strikes from sluggish redfish is to cast a lure over a clump of grass, then jig the lure up and down several times. Finicky redfish will usually fall victim to this yo-yo motion.

5. Muddy water is not all bad. It does not mean that your chance of catching fish is over. It just means that you have to change your approach. Muddy water actually provides some advantages because it positions redfish at a predictable depth. The fish are less spooky, and dark-water redfish are more likely to attack a lure invading their territory than those that can examine it in clear water. If the water is chocolate-colored, the fishing will suffer, but if it is a little off-colored, you may be in luck.

Chapter Seven

Crankin' for Reds:

Crankbaits are my favorite lure for catching redfish when the fish get a little finicky.

Yes crankbaits.

These highly versatile lures can allow anglers seeking redfish a level of precision crucial to catching spooky fish and offer an amazing ability cover large tracts of water in a short order. Those traits have earned crankbaits a permanent place in my saltwater tackle box as a frequent tool in the pursuit of redfish.

JETTY CRANKIN'

Jetty systems hold the biggest redfish and they are not always in an aggressive feeding mode.

"You would be surprised how many redfish you can find still hanging around the jetties throughout the year," said redfish expert Bill Killian.

"And over the years we have found crankbaits to be an important tool for catching them."

Killian said he starts his fishing around the boat cuts in the jetty systems to take advantage of reds foraging on baitfish dispersed from the bays after big cold fronts.

"The boat cuts are a good place to start because during tidal movements you have a lot of baitfish moving through. The boats cuts in a jetty system are the point with the most intense tidal flow because they are a small opening. You will get lots of shrimp, shad and crabs pushing through and the reds will move lie in wait."

Killian said this is a great spot to throw large lipless crankbaits like a Rat-L-Trap.

"Do your best to anchor up current of the cut and work the lure against the current. Let it sink down and then reel it in as fast as you can. The pressure of the current will allow the rattles to work really well."

"Something else you can do is simply lower the lure down and let it flow back with the current. You can get strikes like that too."

Another great spot to find bull reds at the jetties any time are the deep holes usually found around the southern tip of the rocks and back about 50 yards. These spots are where the current wraps around the rocks and carves out large holes.

The reds in these areas tend to move through in small schools or hold over one piece of rock in large numbers.

I use large, lipless crankbaits like the Bomber Saltwater Grade Super Pogy and start by seeking out menhaden (shad) suspended over submerged rocks. The key here is to look for the "cover on the cover". In other words the jetties themselves represent a type of cover but the fish will bond to certain kids. Reds tend to like large boulders that have fallen of the main wall holes carved into the rocks by the current.

Once I locate the bait on these spots, I throw out the Super Pogy, let it sink down to the level of the baitfish and rip it. I will pull a few feet, reel. Pull a few feet and reel. Most of the times the reds will hit just after the first pull and will even hit on the fall.

Something to keep in mind, if there are dolphins feeding in the area consider fortunate. In my logbook, I have noted that every time I have caught lots of bull reds there have been dolphins feeding in the vicinity. The few times we had few fish there were no dolphins feeding. The presence of dolphins is a great indicator of the presence of menhaden which in my opinion is the key to crankbait success on redfish at the jetties.

CHANNEL REDS

Another option for big reds on crankbaits are in the Intracoastal from the just past the Gulf and upwards of two miles north. If you run this area on your depth finder, you will notice large pods of baitfish that sort of stack up. Most of the time it is menhaden but often it can be mullet. Both will draw in these big reds, which tend to suspend below the bait.

Deep diving crankbaits are the key here as these reds will suspend as deep as 20 feet of water. Anglers can cast smaller crankbaits or use trolling plugs ran through the baitfish schools at a medium pace.

If you do not want to troll for these fish, drifting is a viable option. Drop some marker buoys around the baitfish schools and then drift over them while throwing the diving crankbaits. Be very mindful of the depth you are getting struck and mark. Most of the times these reds will be in a very specific area and may not deviate even a few feet.

RIVER REDFISH

A highly under fished area are the river systems north of the bays along the Gulf Coast. They are loaded with redfish and often time huge ones.

These reds tend to roam in small "wolf packs" and feed along riprap, docks and drop-offs. These reds will not always feed aggressively on the surface which is why it is important to wear polarized shades and watch for reds pushing wakes or simply sitting around key pieces of cover.

For sub-surface feeding schools, I use the Super Pogy High Pitch. It mimics the red's primary prey species and can be fished by ripping through the water or letting it sink and over structure and reeling it quickly to the surface.

In these river zones, there is frequently coastal marsh pouring into the rivers and intersected by large manmade canals. Reds use these canals as travel corridors and find feeding easy as tides dump from the marsh to the bays.

Target the areas where these canals empty large marsh ponds or dump into a bay on outgoing tides. Reds gather in the deepest holes and absolutely hammer the menhaden, shrimp and crabs coming out of the marsh. These canals typically range from 3-6 feet deep and where you have adjoining canals or the edge of a pond, tidal flow creates potholes. They can be as shallow as six inches or as deep as two feet and they are like magnets for reds.

These are great places to fish square-billed crankbaits which are perfect for shallow water and can cover lots of water which is key in these kinds of ecosystems. Simply throw them out and reel them in as fast as possible. Most are designed to "walk" most efficiently at a high rate of speed.

Anglers should keep in mind that reds have what can best be described as a "cone of vision"; a term that was first coined by late outdoor writer/redfish guru Ed Holder. Reds can see about 180 degrees and the most likely strikes will be found in front of the red and perhaps just off to the side. If you have a visual on the reds, remember precision casting is important because they will rarely turn around to strike at something they only hear.

Throw just ahead of them or right behind and reel past for best results.

THE RIGHT ROD

Anglers can fish crankbaits on virtually any kind of medium-heavy rod, even on spinning gear although that is not recommended.

The true secret however I learned by fishing with 4-time Bassmaster Classic champion and my all-time fishing hero Rick Clunn.

"Super sensitive rods will actually work against you when fishing with crankbaits. A fish will actually 'push' the lure as they pursue it and if you are fishing a super sensitive (graphite/composite) rod you will set the hook before the fish actually has the lure," Clunn said.

As bass fishing legend Rick Clunn says, a rod that is too sensitive can work against you, whether you are after bass or redfish.

Clunn was speaking of bass when he gave me this information, but I immediately transferred the concept to redfish, and it works.

Clunn collaborated with Wright & McGill to create S-Glass Series of rods that use old fiberglass technology with modern flare. These are the rods I use for my crankbait action and have had serious success everywhere from the Mississippi River near Venice, La. to the Sabine Jetties on the Texas/Louisiana border. There are numerous fiberglass crankbait rods on the market now and they can make a huge difference in the pursuit of redfish.

Redfish are far from dumb fish that will hit anything. Anyone who has truly pursued them for any length of time knows they can be quite challenging which is why crankbaits are crucial for the coastal angler.

They allow a level of precision fishing, not possible with any other kind of lure and that makes a bull redfish sized difference.

Chapter Eight

Stealth Techniques:
Fly-fishing, kayaks and clandestine wading

Catching a redfish with fly-fishing gear is almost too much fun for one person to stand. It is part of what I call "stealth techniques" that allow close contact with these sometimes-spooky fish.

As noted in my previous book, *Texas Trout Tactics*, I am not a fly-fishing expert, but I do enjoy participating in the sport from time to time and there is no inland saltwater fish accessible to Gulf Coast anglers that provides more intense action that redfish.

The generous people at Orvis recommend the following for fly gear selection.

Step 1: Find the proper line weight. Generally, the line weight determines the size of the fly you can accurately cast. Line weights come in sizes 1 through 14, with 1 the lightest. Most anglers use lighter lines for smaller fish in smaller water. Conversely, when fishing large rivers and saltwater, you would go to heavier lines to throw larger flies. Decide where and what you are fishing for and choose a line in that category.

Fly-fishing is a delicate sport that can make for adrenaline-pumping action.

Step 2: Like line, rods come in various "weights" that must match the line weight. Beyond that, choose a rod length appropriate for the venue. Large rivers and saltwater offer you the opportunity to cast aggressively and use a longer rod. Longer rods also help greatly in situations where reaching and mending line are necessary. Saltwater anglers generally use 9- to 9-1/2-foot rods for big open water.

Step 3: Choose your flex. It is largely a matter of personal preference, but it is important. If you choose to use Orvis gear, a new technique called the Orvis Flex Index makes this choice easier than ever. After two years of work, Orvis engineers have developed a numerical method and a scale to quantify the flex pattern of each rod that Orvis manufactures. Every Orvis fly rod has its flex index stamped right on the rod along with the length and weight. It will soon become one of the most important factors in your search for the right fly rod. According to Orvis, this process is very simple:

> Let's say you have a 5-weight that you love dearly, and think is the finest casting tool ever built. Now you need a 10-weight and you want the same familiar and comfortable action.
>
> Before Flex Index was developed, it would have required a long and laborious quest, casting a number of rods, trying to find that one rod that casts like your 10-weight. With the new Orvis Flex Index, that problem is eliminated.
>
> You can now walk to the rack and find the rod that is labeled with the identical or closest number on the flex scale to the rod you like. Its casting properties will be similar if not identical. Most anglers will not notice a difference in rod action unless the Flex Index varies by two points or more. This will hold true for any length and weight rod you decide you need.
>
> Each Orvis rod can now be identified as a full flex, mid flex, or tip flex rod, and can be narrowed down even further within those designations to an absolute number.

PERSONAL CHOICES AND FLY PATTERNS

The way I see it, purchasing fly-fishing gear is another scenario where you get what you pay for. If you plan on trying this sport, you might want to get an inexpensive saltwater combo, but if you are really into it, more expensive gear is required. Not all fly-fishing tackle is equal, but if you are an expert, I do not need to tell you this; you could teach me a few things about the sport.

Nowadays, anglers have a huge variety of flies to choose from, many of which are as effective as they are colorful.

CLOUSER MINNOW: Most saltwater fly-fishermen say if they had to choose only one fly for all their fishing, this would be it. It is great in the shallows and in deep water. I caught my first redfish on a chartreuse/white variation. I also caught my first speckled trout on it.

HALF/HALF: This shrimp imitation is a heavy sinking fly that requires a slow-to-fast action. This makes it resemble a shrimp's herky-jerky actions. MUDDLER MINNOW: Some call this the "all-time classic redfish fly." It resembles a minnow and is responsible for catching many redfish, particularly in Florida, where it is very popular.

DECEIVER MENHADEN: This is another popular fly, and one I have fished in No. 5/0 with a white and pink pattern. BAY ANCHOVY: There are many of good patterns of small translucent baitfishes to choose. These are great because they come in many sizes and can help you "match the hatch." You can get these from 1/2-inch up to 3 inches long.

LEFTY'S DECEIVER: This fly is named after fly-fishing legend Lefty Kreh, and often produces when others will not. It is very popular among fly-fishing enthusiasts, particularly in Florida.

POPPERS: Poppers are fun to fish with because they are the topwater plugs of the fly-fishing world. Enough said.

PRESENTATION

Casting to reds means getting the fly close to the fish and into its "cone of vision," as discussed elsewhere in this book. The key is casting close enough so that it sees the fly but does not spook. Lead the fish by 10 feet so that you can strip the fly to intersect its path.

When a redfish strikes your fly, use a firm, strip-strike when you feel the hit. Do not strike directly up the rod, because if the redfish has the fly, it may come shooting out of the water. Some anglers prefer a firm rod strike to the side. It is best to keep your rod tip high while forming a circle with your left forefinger and thumb to smoothly clear the line. Now you can concentrate on landing the fish. Keep the rod tip high so you can avoid getting the line snapped on underwater obstructions. This includes grass, which can easily accumulate on the line.

KAYAKS

A growing number of coastal anglers are using kayaks to maneuver in bay, lagoon, and surf systems. These lightweight crafts may look like something out of an Alaska wilderness film, but they are highly effective right here on the Gulf Coast, where the sand meets the surf.

Kayaks are sleek, quiet crafts that allow anglers to get literally right on top of fish without spooking them. Another issue kayaks address is fishing access. Many coastal anglers do not own boats, and most of the time that is due to finances. A new bay boat can cost $50,000 and more, while a kayak can cost

PHOTO BY CHARLES DUKES

Flyfishing expert Phil Shook pulls a kayak through marsh on the Gulf Coast somewhere. Kayaks are great for getting into areas otherwise inaccessible by motorboats.

under $1,000. Sure, a bay boat while take an angler greater distances in a shorter time, but kayaks allow anglers to get into spots motor boats simply cannot go. It takes only a few inches of water for a kayak to remain afloat. Some of the best spots to kayak are tidal lakes, tidal flats, and remote salt marsh lakes.

The kayak can open a whole new world to the fisherman whose bay rig needs 1 to 2 feet of water to navigate safely and comfortably. Some of these salt marsh lakes are 6 inches deep in spots, but they hold many fish. Also, many of these areas are located a short distance from bank fishing spots, where a quick trip in a kayak could put the angler into area no one else can go. In the world of redfishing, that is a real plus.

Because kayaks are much smaller and lighter than other craft, they pose safety issue beyond those of other boaters. Here are some kayak safety tips from the Maine Island Trail Association, a group dedicated to safe kayaking and other outdoor activities.

Always take:

• a kayak in good, serviceable condition, with plenty of secure buoyancy, fore and aft
• a paddle
• spray cover that fits your boat
• personal flotation device and whistle
• clothing suitable for all conditions
• bailer or pump
• accessible spare paddle, minimum 1 per group

In any but the most benign conditions, also consider:

• accessible flare pack
• flashlight (even for day trips)
• self-rescue aids

- rain gear and extra clothing in a waterproof bag
- minimum of 25 feet of towline
- charts and tide tables
- compass
- knife
- matches or a lighter
- first aid kit
- weather radio

PRECAUTIONS FOR BEGINNERS

- familiarize yourself with your boat
- start gradually in moderate weather, close to shore, and with an experienced companion.
- develop your paddling skills, turning, and bracing
- carry safety equipment
- leave a float plan
- get a weather forecast before you go out each day
- know the principles of navigation and seamanship
- watch out for other watercraft and know right-of-way (a larger vessel always has the right-of-way)

WADE-FISHING

Sometimes, it simply pays to get in the water with the redfish. This is an especially good method when a falling tide reveals redfish actively feeding in the shallows with their tails or dorsal fins sticking out of the water. At these times, the fish can be caught by sight-casting.

While wading for reds, it is important to dress properly. Quality wade-fishing belts, like the Wade-Aid, provide superior back support and plenty of places to carry gear. Walking through water can tire muscles quickly and

Wade-fishing requires good gear and a willingness to stay in the water despite the presence of everything from stingrays to sharks.

cause back pain in anglers even in the best of shape.

During winter months, neoprene waders are a must-have item. Catching redfish is cool and everything, but hypothermia is not—no pun intended. Wade-fishermen face other hazards. Rip currents are the most threatening natural hazard along our coast. They pull victims away from the beach. The United States Lifesaving Association has found that 80 percent of the rescues affected by ocean lifeguards involve saving those caught in rip currents.

A rip current is a seaward moving current that circulates water back to sea after the waves push it ashore. Each wave accumulates water on shore, creating seaward pressure. This pressure releases in an area with the least amount of resistance, which is usually the deepest point along the ocean floor. Rip currents also exist in areas where objects such as rock jetties, piers, natural reefs, and even large groups of bathers weaken the waves. Rip currents often look like muddy rivers flowing away from shore.

Rip currents are sometimes mistakenly called "rip tides" or "undertows." These are misnomers. Rip currents are not directly associated with tides and they do not pull people under.

Try to avoid wading where rip currents are present. If you become caught in one, swim parallel to the shore until the pull stops, and then swim back to shore. If you are unable to return to the beach, tread water, and try to attract the attention of your fishing partner—never wade-fish alone. Stay at least 100 feet away from piers and jetties; rip currents often exist along the side of fixed objects in the water. Clearly, wade-fishing is not for everyone.

To those who have never seriously pursued wade-fishing, you may consider it strange to soak oneself in saltwater and face hazards like stingrays, when boats offer more comfort and the ability to cover more ground more quickly—but that is exactly what dedicated waders do not like.

From my standpoint, I see stealth as a very important aspect of wading. Because walking in saltwater can be flat out tough, wading forces the angler to fish slower and look at an area differently. Being in a more intimate relationship with your surroundings creates a different perspective, and sometimes that is what it takes to get anglers to see the little things that can lead to a limit.

Chapter Nine

F.L.E.X.ing for Monster Reds

Fishing has always been about fun for me. I have never engaged in competitive angling or even been much on bragging on big catches. There is certainly nothing wrong with either but my interest in fishing comes from the experience side.

A few years ago, however, I became intensely fascinated with big fish. I do not necessarily mean marlin or tuna or other aquatic giants but the biggest specimens of any species I pursue. It did not matter if they were crappie or bull sharks, I just wanted to understand more about the giants among them.

Through nearly two decades of outdoor writing and lifelong study of fish, I realized there was something different about the really big fish of any given species. Very different.

There is a reason a flounder attains a 24-inch length in a state like Texas where there are 800,000 rod-and-reelers on the coast and both recreational and commercial anglers pursuing them with lights and gigs at night. Something is imbedded in the DNA of those fish that make them not only grow to giant proportions but avoid harvest.

The author has caught hundreds of giant redfish like this one using principles in the F.L.E.X. *system.*

Similar and even more impressive statistics can be given for largemouth bass, speckled trout and virtually any other species pursued in the United States of America. Big fish are special by virtue of not only their size but also their elusiveness.

Having fished all over the world over the years I have been blessed to experience some truly big fish. Some of them were caught by chance, others by focused effort and others because I am an outdoors writer and people like to put us on big fish. Guides and chambers of commerce know it is good business to put members of the outdoor media on huge fish, so we get lots of invites. I find nothing at all wrong with this, but I like to be honest about it and publicly recognize the fact we get some golden opportunities.

It might be more comfortable acting like that is not a reality, but I have made a vow to never let any level of dishonesty creep into my writing even if it is simply through omission. With that said, I began to wonder if there was a way anglers might be able to systematically target and catch big fish whether they are a spoiled outdoor writer or someone who can barely afford a fishing license.

You see I know what it is like to live my outdoors dreams. When I was a kid from a lower-middle income family in Orange, TX, I would to sit in my Dad's lap and cut out photos from outdoors magazines we would buy at the thrift store.

I had one for fishing and one for hunting. Dad and I would sit and talk about the dreams we had to pursue them.

I have been blessed beyond measure to get to catch many of the fish I used to collect clippings of and have had plenty of "pinch me" moments on the water.

Whether it was catching peacock bass in South America or huge specked trout in the marshes of Louisiana I have lived an amazing life from a fisherman's perspective.

During this exhaustive study of big fish I began to toy with the idea of creating a system for anglers to follow to catch their dream fish. It had to be something anyone could do from a financial perspective and that included the all- important aspect of experience. I never value a fish by its weight or length just as I do not value a whitetail deer by the number of antlers hanging on its head. I do however know how exciting it is to fight and land a big, elusive fish and the kind of smiles it can produce.

Fish are fun to catch but big fish are really fun to catch.

If I could find a way to create good business opportunities for me that legitimately helped anglers, I thought maybe it was something truly worth pursuing.

Enter F.L.E.X. Focus. Learn. Eliminate. Experience.

I asked the Lord to grant me the knowledge to help people in their fishing and suddenly incredible information was coming my way via opportunities to fish and interview the world's top anglers. They were seemingly a weekly occurrence. I knew He had His hand in this, so I took my time, prayed even more, thought it all out and finally put it to the test.

I want you to catch the fish of your dreams and in this case the redfish of your dreams. I want you to help that childhood wish of landing a bull red so big you can barely hold it up for a snapshot. That is fun stuff and is something I guarantee F.L.E.X. will help you do.

FOCUS

Dreams. The F.L.E.X. system begins in the realm of dreams.

I believe all angling dreams are attainable within reason.

I say "within reason" because some people get way too specific on how they want to catch a certain kind of trophy fish. I have heard of people saying things like, "My dream is to catch a 30-inch speckled trout wade fishing on the southern shoreline of Baffin Bay while throwing a bone-colored She Dog."

Really?

Why don't you pick the exact weight and then decide if you want the fish to slurp the plug under or give you a vicious blowup too? That would really impress the guys at work.

Those kinds of statements are typically made by anglers who have no real intentions of ever going the extra mile to pursue their dream fish and would rather put up a bunch of qualifying obstacles to make it easy on them.

I guarantee you if they caught a big trout on a live mullet under a popping cork they would be just as happy. However, if they go fishing all the time and never get that big fish, their list of hurdles to overcome makes it seem like they are on task when in reality they are most likely focused on their own insecurities.

I can go with someone saying his or her dream is to catch a trout bigger than 25 inches on a topwater on Lake Calcasieu or a 30-incher in Baffin Bay. Both of those are attainable and fit into the F.LE.X. framework but when you start adding a bunch of specifics you lose focus.

The first step of F.L.E.X. is to focus on your angling dream. To focus on your dream fish and reconcile within yourself what would make you happy as an angler and what would be fun to pursue is very important.

If you are reading this because you want to be the next Kevin Van Dam, or you want to show your buddies at work that you can fish as good as them stop now. This is not what F.L.E.X. is about.

Professional, competitive angling is a whole other kind of fishing and although many F.L.E.X. principles apply, it is a different game and one I do not pretend to master. Study the pros if you want to do that kind of thing, not my philosophy.

And if you are in this to prove something to someone other than yourself, you are doing this for the wrong reason.

In my opinion, the only reason to pursue something like fishing is to 1. Give glory to God. 2. Because you have a genuine passion for it. 3. To make money.

Trying to win the acceptance and approval of others is an empty pursuit and one that is a huge problem among anglers. It never gets written about, but the fact is lots of people (especially men) who are really into fishing weigh their personal value on the fish they catch. If this is you, I am not pointing the finger of judgment but instead offering you some freedom and a new lease on your angling life.

Go back to your childhood and remember what drove you to fish to begin with. It might have been watching Bill Dance land a monster bucket-mouthed bass on television or seeing your Dad bringing home a bull redfish from the beach. There is no question every angler wants to catch big fish and if you really tap into your early angling memories you can probably find unfulfilled fishing dreams.

And yet some anglers like myself would simply like to take our fishing to the next level and experience the catching super-sized elusive specimens of a variety of species on a regular basis. You will learn more about this aspect soon, but it is a legitimate reason for taking up F.L.E.X.

Focus on a realistic goal you would like to attain and your journey into the F.L.E.X. system begins.

This should not be too difficult.

What is it you are truly hoping is on the other end of your line when you set the hook? That is what your focus should be.

At this time in history trying to break world records, state records and that sort of thing is pointless. Most records other than specific water body or line class records are monster fish that catching has as much to do with chance as it did skill. Think about the largemouth bass record, which stood for more than 70 years and was recently tied by a Japanese angler. There have been literally hundreds of millions of people fish for bass since the first record was caught spending billions of hours on the water and it took seven decades for someone to tie it.

However, out of those huge number of anglers millions of trophy-sized largemouth have been caught and that is what F.L.E.X. is about.

Focus on what you would like to catch and take out a pen right now. Write down the size redfish you want to catch and declare you will catch this fish. You now have an ally in the F.L.E.X. system.

LEARN

The number one reason most anglers never catch the fish of their dreams is they know very little about them.

In my career I am blessed to meet thousands of anglers a year and correspond with thousands more via e-mail, social networking and my radio program. Despite being conscientious, caring and passionate about fishing, most of them possess very little knowledge of the species they pursue.

If I had to grade these anglers on fish knowledge based on grade school levels, the average would be somewhere around fifth grade.

This may sound harsh but the point of the F.L.E.X. system is to show you how to catch more big fish, the kind you have been dreaming about your whole life. To attain this requires an open and honest look at the things holding us back and fish knowledge is a big part of this.

Fish knowledge can be defined as understanding intimate details of the life history and biology of a given species. And attaining it requires more than what Pawpaw taught you. He may have given you the basics and even some really good tactics but in most cases, Pawpaw did not know a whole lot about what really makes fish tick.

The F.L.E.X. Fishing system was developed by the author to help anglers have a simple to learn system to catch their dream fish.

Owning this book is a major first step in educating yourself about redfish. I have done the research for you but there is more.

The first place is on the water. It is really hard to beat what you can see and touch, so look at each fishing trip as an educational opportunity from the time you get on the water to the cleaning station (if you end up there).

I believe in keeping fishing logs and there will soon be F.L.E.X. logs that detail the component of this system in an easy to document format. Even scribbling down small notes can reveal F.L.E.X. principles that will help you gain major insight into fish.

Here is a sample from a trip to seek bull reds at the Sabine Jetties. It comes from the additional notes section of my personal fishing log.

"For the first time the dolphins weren't here. And for the first time we did not catch a single bull red. No mullet or big shad here either."

What does that tell you about the fish? The thing that jumps out at me the most is there seemed to be a direct correlation between a lack of dolphins and a lack of baitfish. That in turns ended up with no bull redfish or any redfish for that matter.

Sometimes the best way to catch the biggest fish is by going where others don't go. Kayaks can allow anglers to reach spots where some of the biggest inland reds dwell and powerboats don't.

This particular spot has given up hundreds of 30 plus redfish over the years and only on two occasions have we not caught oversized reds here. On both of those occasions there were no dolphins. Now when traveling to different locations we know that locating dolphins feeding on the edge of a jetty often equals bull redfish presence.

You can also learn a lot about fish by cleaning them. I have examined the stomach contents of most fish I have cleaned since I have been a little boy.

Whether it was the stomach totally full of small blue crabs in a ling or the sand eels in speckled trout, I learned something about the fish that could directly apply to catching them.

The knowledge to greatly alter my tackle in relation to the nearly impenetrable skull of a flounder came from drying out some of their skulls and discussing this with a friend who did the same thing. Do not be afraid to dissect and study what you catch.

ELIMINATE

This is the heart of the F.L.E.X. system. It is the means by which you begin to move from knowledge to experience.

Elimination is the difference between catching fish and catching BIG fish.

And it is crucial that you spend some time reflecting on this aspect of F.L.E.X. and apply it to your fishing.

Once you have focused on your fishing dream and learned about the species you choose to pursue it is time to eliminate the things that can keep you from it. And there are lots of them. Let us use largemouth bass for as an example. Say an angler named Ted has decided to pursue the lifelong dream of catching a 10-pound largemouth bass. Seeing one caught on television fishing show is what got him hooked on the sport to begin with and he has decided it is time to finally feel one on the end of his line, hold it is in hands and take a snapshot for the photo album.

The first thing he needs to consider is his location.

Ted fishes exclusively at Fayette County Reservoir and that is a problem to begin with. While there are nice fish there and lots of them, there are not nearly enough to justify focusing efforts there in the F.L.E.X. system. The statistics simply do not bear it out.

The Texas Parks & Wildlife Department has a program called Sharelunker that seeks donations of live bass weighing 13 pounds or more for spawning purposes. Since the program's inception in 1986, Fayette has produced no Sharelunkers. Nearby Sam Rayburn, however, has produced 23 making it the number 3 lake in overall Sharelunker production. It does not take a genius to figure out if it can consistently produce 13-pounders there are plenty of 10-pounders around. In fact, a simple search of tournament results on the lake make this crystal clear.

It is not that Fayette County is a bad lake to fish. In fact, the fishing there is great. However, in using the F.L.E.X. system to step up from catching fish

When seeking big fish use baits or lures that attract them. Big spinnerbaits for example rarely catch small redfish.

to catching BIG fish, the first process of elimination is targeting water bodies where you dream fish are more likely to dwell. And although the lake record there is 12.25 pound it was caught way back in 1982. This is not the sign of the lake that is going to have a large proportion of 10-pounders.

By sticking a little closer to home and fishing Rayburn, Ted could make a giant leap toward attaining his lifelong angling goal. Don't you think that would be worth it?

Elimination is the part of the system an angler can take as far as he or she wants to get closer to making their dream a reality.

With that said, if Ted were to really want to jumpstart his dream angling quest, he would schedule a few trips per year to Lake Fork which is only three more hours away and has produced 246 Sharelunkers. In fact, if he did further research, he would learn a voluntary angler survey conducted at Lake Fork marinas shows an average of about 500 10-pound plus fish reported there annually.

Instead of making 15 trips a year to Fayette County he could do 10 to Rayburn and 5 to Fork and exponentially increase his opportunity of catching that 10-pounder. If he followed this system, he could without a doubt achieve his goal in short order and experience other beautiful waterways in the process.

I have developed a five point system for selecting a location. If you can line up at least three of these, you are in good shape and are stand a decent chance of realizing your new F.L.E.X. goal. If you line up four or more, you are well on your way.

Here is how to do so for redfish.

1. History: A water body with a history of producing big fish of the variety you prefer is an obvious for what you are looking to accomplish. If you find an area with either a consistent history of producing monster redfish in line with a recent history trending toward big fish, you are in good shape. If an angler wanted to catch a 45 plus inch redfish, he could study an area like the nearshore Gulf out to Corpus Christi. However, when looking at recent history it would become obvious that fishery has declined in trophy production in recent years and chances of catching a fish of that size are not as great as they could be. Sure there are lots of 36 plus inch reds there, but giants are rare.

If you however looked into Venice, La. you would see that area has a rich history of producing reds of that size and while they are still not an everyday catch down there, such fish are present and definitely catchable.

2. Management: An area not managed for big fish will not consistently produce big fish. There is simply too much intelligent angling pressure out there to make this possible in most of the continental United States. Finding an area with good redfish management is a good start. Many areas on the Texas coast have good management as do areas in Florida. Louisiana has some of the most lax redfish laws but they make up for it with having the largest chunk of marsh on the Gulf Coast. Marsh produces redfish so if you are looking for big reds, look for marshes that are well managed, not just the actual fish. The marshes around Venice, La. I mentioned are very well managed by the way.

3. Pressure: This ties in with two types of location: water body and specific spots on a water body. Nowadays it is rare to find a water body that produces lots of big fish that is lightly pressured. In the information age, people find out about big catches in real time and respond accordingly. A dream scenario is a water body that gets very little angling pressure and fishing a kind of specific location on it that gets even less. I fish a stretch of distant bayou in the Louisiana marsh for reds and rarely see other anglers. Even fewer are targeting the deeper cuts I focus on and it in turn produces lots of big fish. These places are rare but special.

Thad Daly used the F.L.E.X. principles to catch this huge red in the Sabine River while fishing with the author.

4. Seasonality: Fish are driven by a variety of seasonal urges and timing in particular areas that can literally enhance the chance of catching monster fish tenfold. Probably the greatest example is with redfish which we cover in depth in another chapter. The huge spawning-sized specimens congregate in the near shore Gulf in late summer and early fall in large numbers. There will sometimes be literal acres of them. By targeting these areas during the spawn period the chances of catching the fish of a lifetime are off the charts.

5. Phenomenon: This is the wild card of our destination selection process. Natural phenomena occur that can be extremely valuable in your quests. They are not common but when they happen, you need to be on the water. Tropical storms provide by far the best action for giant redfish. They go absolutely crazy when a storm is in the Gulf and hit the beach front with vigor. Please do not take any crazy risks to catch them but if they area you live in is getting higher tides than normal and maybe just a little rain, there is no better time to get a truly huge red.

This elimination principle is not limited to location. It also applies to lures, baits and presentation.

Once an angler has focused on a goal, studied the habits of that species and selected a high percentage location to target them, it is now time to eliminate small specimens and non-target species. The fact you are pursuing a wild creature you in most cases cannot see that is in competition with a large variety of other fish makes catching trophy fish a challenge. You need to focus on baits and lures that will rule out a large chunk of the competition.

When I pursue bull redfish, I typically fish for them at deep holes around jetties where they tend to congregate in small schools of giant specimens. Most of the time I fish is during late summer and early fall and these areas are loaded with sharks, stingrays, gafftopsail catfish, hardhead catfish, Spanish mackerel and a host of other fish that vie for a lot of the same food.

Over a 15-year span I have fished one particular location over 100 times and NOT caught bull redfish over 40 inches on three of them due to using the F.L.E.X. principles.

Until recently I did not realize I was using a system that would forever change my approach to fishing, but I was, and it is a prime example of eliminating competition.

My preferred lure is large live croaker. I use croaker up to about two pounds live and hooked through the nose, fished on an extra-large Carolina rig on the bottom.

This eliminates all hardhead catfish, 99 percent of gafftopsail catfish, most stingrays and a large portion of sharks.

Cut bait works great for reds but if there are sharks in the area, they will hit it before the reds can ever get there. Fishing it on the bottom of the water column eliminates a lot of sharks as well as many of the blacktips and spinners in the area feed in the upper half.

In addition this eliminates small redfish. Out of literally hundreds of redfish caught in this location over the years, using giant croaker and mullet occasionally I have caught one red that was under 36 inches. Big bait does truly equal big fish and eliminates many non-target species and small ones of the species you are after.

I conducted a seminar about fishing options for the landbound angler on the Texas Gulf Coast. The first thing I said is if you want to catch legal-sized speckled trout, redfish and flounder do not fish with shrimp.

I got a stunned look because nearly every landbound angler fishes with shrimp and for good reason. It catches everything, but that is the problem. Most of these same anglers were complaining about problems catching legal-sized fish as they either catch hardheads and croaker all day or under-sized game fish. The problem is the bait.

I told them to let their kids fish with shrimp, throw back the hardheads, tie on the live croaker the kids catch for bait and bring a cast net to catch mullet, mud minnows or any kind of finfish for live bait and the odds of catching legal-sized gamefish go up dramatically. This is a F.L.E.X. elimination principle. Forget targeting the masses of fish, you are after the upper classes of fish.

EXPERIENCE

Experience is by far the most important element in the F.L.E.X. system. It is the means by which we transcend the unrealistic expectations placed upon us by the world and enter into the realm of our very own dreams.

The catalyst for F.L.E.X. was initially a desire to catch larger bass which led to these fishing principles soon applied to species ranging from flounder to crappie and the realization they could work for all fish.

The root of my desire to catch bigger bass than the ones I had been catching was much deeper.

Experience is the "X" in F.L.E.X. and is all about passing on what you have learned and savoring the opportunity God has given you. The author has alway admired anglers like Rick Clunn who not only talk about the catch or in his case win but what he experienced on the water.

It was not to achieve bragging rights, to cross of a goal sworn years previous or anything of the like.

I wanted to feel the fish's powerful strike and watch its deep red gills flare as it opened its gaping mouth while furiously leaping from the water. I wanted to feel its weight, the curvature of its muscles and gaze upon its scale pattern as I held it in my hands. In other words, I wanted to know the fish.

Whitetail bowhunters probably understand this more than any other sector of the outdoors community. I have spoken with men who have dozens of legitimate monster bucks to their credit who have told me the greatest joy they get from the harvest is knowing the animal well enough to be able to release an arrow.

A person can learn a lot about deer by photographing or simply observing them but not until they become their predator can one truly know the animal. Taking a snapshot is one thing but to be able to go into the woods and specifically target a big buck requires a whole other level of knowledge. It involves the ability to get beyond their amazing senses to within 30 yards, draw back a bow and guide an arrow to the right spot.

That is why I believe the ultimate example of knowing a fish is to fool it into biting. And the ultimate knowledge of a species can be gained from pursuing its largest specimens. As we discussed earlier, fish of great size are special representatives of their species, representing a tiny fraction of the overall population. It took many factors coinciding for them to get to this level. If you get to know them the rest are a piece of cake and your angling excursions will undoubtedly be far more productive.

I remember looking at one of those thick fishing annual magazines that used to be popular when I was a little boy. They were book-sized and always featured a variety of articles on numerous species and of course plenty of gratuitous big fish shots.

My grandmother used to take me to the local thrift shop to peruse the magazines, which were only a nickel apiece, and I would wipe out all that had to do with hunting and fishing. Right before we left to visit relatives in Tennessee one year, I picked up one of these annuals and brought it along to keep me occupied on the road. It had great stories about sailfish and walleye and redfish but something about a particular bass story blew me away.

It was probably the shot of a man holding a 12-pounder with its gigantic mouth aimed toward the camera with a backdrop of a lily pad-covered lake that did it. I had recently found a spot near my home that looked very similar.

Could a monster like the one in this story lurk there? If so, how might I catch it? Would my little Beetle Spins work or would I need to something else entirely?

These questions raced through my mind from the time we left the coastal plains of Texas until we reached the Smoky Mountains and back. I never did catch a big bass there, but I still think about it every time I drive by. If I had understood these principles at that young age, I would have had a much better understanding and saved my allowance money for a trip to Lake Fork instead of buying an armada of lures thrown to little avail in a lily pad-covered rice canal.

Still I think that whole experience played into this book being in your hands today. The dreams implanted into us as children are from the Lord himself and I have a feeling He knew that one day He would have a writer on His hands with me and that would be able to help show others how to maximize their angling experience.

It is important for us to pursue dreams and encounter things that give us joy. God put these creatures on Earth for our benefit and gave us dominion over them for a reason. All positive things come from Him and all good feelings that run deep into our souls are divinely inspired.

Do yourself a favor and tap into the dreams of your youth. Or if fishing is new to you embrace the concept of getting to know big fish and find joy in understanding their most secret habits. Use this system to allow you to hold that huge speckled trout you salivated over as a kiddo or catch that lunker largemouth that got you to buy a boat in the first place. Tap into the experience and see your angling life changed forever.

Mine has been and I thought I had already lived out most of mine.

Ha!

F.L.E.X. has allowed me to see this is only just the beginning and this is coming from someone who has caught everything from giant sturgeon to wahoo. If it can change my life, I know it can yours.

Avoid at all costs using the fish you catch as a status symbol or means to outdo your co-workers, brother-in-law or someone else you have some sort of competition with. The only legitimate competition for fishing involves tournaments where money is exchanged, all others a fix for gaps in self-esteem or a form of vanity.

There is nothing at all wrong with a little bragging but if you have made it this far, I am sure you know the reality of what I am saying.

Flounder

One-ups on other anglers do not fuel the spirit. They only make it crave more of the same, creating a void. The realization of a dream and embracing the pursuit of great fish however can lift the spirit to great heights because it is the kind of thing implanted in us by the one who created all of it to begin with.

I will never recommend fishing so you can watch the sun rise over the water or any other of a dozen clichés common in the outdoor media. Fishing is about catching fish. The other stuff is wonderful but there are cheaper and

Redfish

Speckled trout

less time- consuming ways to see experience those.

There goes that word "experience" again. It is crucial in this process and allows one dream to form another and the cycle to continue. Never think you have climbed all of the mountains because there is always another.

Just like there is a big bull redfish suspended over one of the jagged rocks at my favorite jetty location, there is always an experience to seek. I think I will go practice what I preach and show that fish what F.L.E.X. is all about.

Am I that confident? You bet.

And if you follow these principles you should be too. I will leave you with photos of fish caught using F.L.E.X. from May 15, 2010 through June 29, 2010. In that period I was able to catch redfish, largemouth bass, speckled trout, flounder and crappie that were in the top five biggest I have caught in 30 plus years of fishing.

Largemouth

Crappie

Chapter Ten

Releasing Redfish

Conservation means the wise use of resources.

With fisheries around the country facing more intelligent pressure than ever, conservation is not only wise it is paramount.

That is why anglers must learn proper catch-and-release strategies.

Releasing fish, particularly, the large breeding-sized fish was first popularized and perfected in the largemouth bass fishery and has transferred with great success throughout all realms of angling.

Although catch-and-release recreational fishing is a modern practice, the basic tent goes back thousands of years.

Ancient Hebrew writings called for the people to only take eggs from ground-nesting birds and to not take the mother.

The ideas was that the mother would lay again and produce more young but when the female was taken, no more were produced. This is essentially the modern practice of taking smaller fish to eat an letting the breeders go.

Of course not all released fish are females, nor should they be but the

It's always best to keep fish in the water as much as possible during catch-and-release. It's not always possible but it is ideal.

fact is without breeders, fisheries will not only decline in terms of fish size but numbers will plummet as well.

And then there is the personal side of catch-and-release.

I am all for catching a mess of crappie for example and frying them up alongside some hush puppies and spending an enjoyable evening with family.

There is however something special about catching a big or particularly elusive fish so it can fight another day.

That is not only good for the species but is good for the spirit and there is a very specific way to release redfish developed by the South Carolina Department of Natural Resources.

• Fish with non-offset circle hooks when fishing with live or natural bait. Bend the barbs down for even faster release times.

• Bring fish in quickly. Do not play fish to exhaustion.

• Release fish quickly. Do not keep fish out of water while you find your camera.

Releasing sub-adult red drum in shallow water:

• Use appropriate tackle (at least 12 lb test fishing line) and bring the fish in quickly. Fighting a fish to exhaustion may increase its possibility of dying.

• Use non-offset CIRCLE HOOKS. (We used Eagle Claw 4/0). This study has shown that circle hooks catch sub-adult red drum in the jaw over 90% of the time. Mortality is 1/5 of that with either offset circle hooks or J-hooks.

• Handle the fish only with wet hands. Use a release tool such as needle-nosed pliers to remove the hook from the mouth of the fish.

• If the point of the hook is lodged in the far back of the mouth or is beyond the crushing teeth in the back of the throat, leave the hook in place and cut the leader. A large proportion of these fish will survive.

Releasing adult red drum in deep water:

• Use appropriate tackle (at least 20 lb test line) and bring the fish in quickly. Remember, these fish are either in the act of spawning or have just recently spawned. This activity alone is EXTREMELY exhausting, and being caught on a hook adds extra stress to an already difficult time.

• Use non-offset CIRCLE HOOKS. (We used Eagle Claw 9/0 or 10/0). This study has shown that over 95 percent of adult red drum caught on Circle hooks are caught in the lip. Two-day mortality is half of what it is with J-hooks.

• Avoid fishing during the hottest part of the summer. Water temperatures can have a profound effect on whether a fish can revive after being caught.

• Handle the fish only with wet hands. Use a release tool such as needle-nosed pliers to remove the hook.

• Release the fish gently. If it is sluggish or floating upside down, allow it to rest for a few moments near the surface. GENTLY move it forward through the water to pass water over the gills. Most fish will regain enough strength to make it to the bottom within a minute or so.

If you plan to release redfish use line heavy enough to bring the fish in quickly. Long fights often equal dead fish.

REDFISH CATCH AND RELEASE WORKS

In the summer of 2001, I was deeply involved in tagging sharks for the Mote Marine Laboratory and Texas Sea Grant.

The Sea Grant folks said if we caught any bull redfish, to go ahead and place a tag in them as well.

While fishing a nearshore gas platform off the coast of Sabine Pass, my friend Bill Killian caught a big bull red, so I quickly broke out the tagging equipment, recorded the information and put it back into the sand-green waters.

Three weeks later, we were fishing the Sabine Jetties which are about two miles away and the line alarm on my reel sounded.

As I grabbed the rod, it bent in two and I soon realized I had on a very big fish.

A few minutes later, a large bull redfish surfaced and Killian netted it on the first run past the boat.

As soon as we put the fish in the boat, I noticed a tag covered with slime.

Being registered in the annual CCA STAR tournament which features tagged redfish that earn anglers a truck, I was stoked, but then I realized they do not tag 40 plus inch reds. They only tag the slot-sized specimens.

As I removed the slime, my heart raced as I realized the tag said Sea Grant. After examining our data, we realized it was the exact same fish Killian caught that I tagged the week before.

What an amazing experience!

It taught me something about redfish movement patterns but more importantly let me know firsthand that releasing big fish pays off. I will carry that with me the rest of my life.

Chapter Eleven

Redfish Hotspots

Anglers seeking redfish have no problem scoring virtually anywhere along the Gulf Coast. Conservation efforts directed at the species have enhanced the fishery to an astounding level, but that does not mean certain spots are not better than others are. Here are the best of the best from Texas and Louisiana.

JACK'S POCKET (TRINITY BAY)

It does not take a PhD to figure out where the redfish are in Trinity Bay during the fall. Besides the splashing and gulping sounds of feeding predatory fish, there are other obvious visual indicators—the water takes on a strange bronze tint.

Jack's Pocket in Trinity Bay is routinely one of the best spots to seek schooling reds. And, yes, there are so many reds in the area that sometimes the water actually turns bronze. Stories of "acres" of reds roaming the shallows spark much excitement among the Upper Coast angling community. Heck, I'm getting excited just writing about it, although I believe the term "acre" may be a slight exaggeration of the size of these schools.

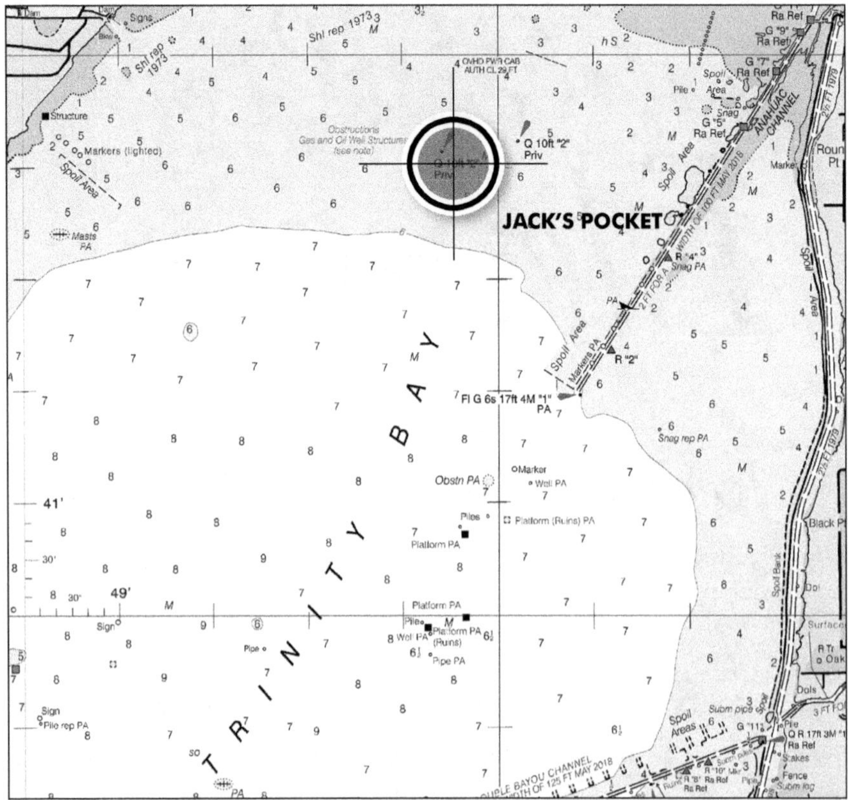

Approximate location of Jack's Pocket on Galveston-Trinity Bay

The intense fish feeding may last for five minutes or an hour. We had an odd, on-again, off-again year on Trinity Bay in 2003, but usually things settle into an easy-to-catch pattern come November. These big redfish schools feed on even larger schools of menhaden and shrimp that are making their exodus to the Gulf. The easiest way to find these frenzy feeding schools is by locating diving gulls picking off the nervous baitfish reds push to the surface. However, do not rely solely on birds to find the fish. Anglers typically throw spoons or soft plastic lures for these reds.

During recent autumns, I have used 12-pound-test and a 3/8- to 1/2-ounce jighead to get past the small trout that often hang around the reds. The little specks feed on top and the reds rove around the bottom. Fish down low to get the biggest and best fish.

It is usually better to drift over these schools than to fish them with a trolling motor. In the past, I have approached these big schools by motoring far away from the school to an up-current position and then drifting through the feeding action.

UPPER LAGUNA MADRE

Upper Laguna Madre is an underrated destination for redfish. Lots of the time this area turns on in early June when light southeasterly winds push clear water up from Port Mansfield. With the clear waters comes good fishing.

Any of the shorelines of the islands adjacent to the ship channel can provide a good topwater bite early in the mornings, especially when the wind

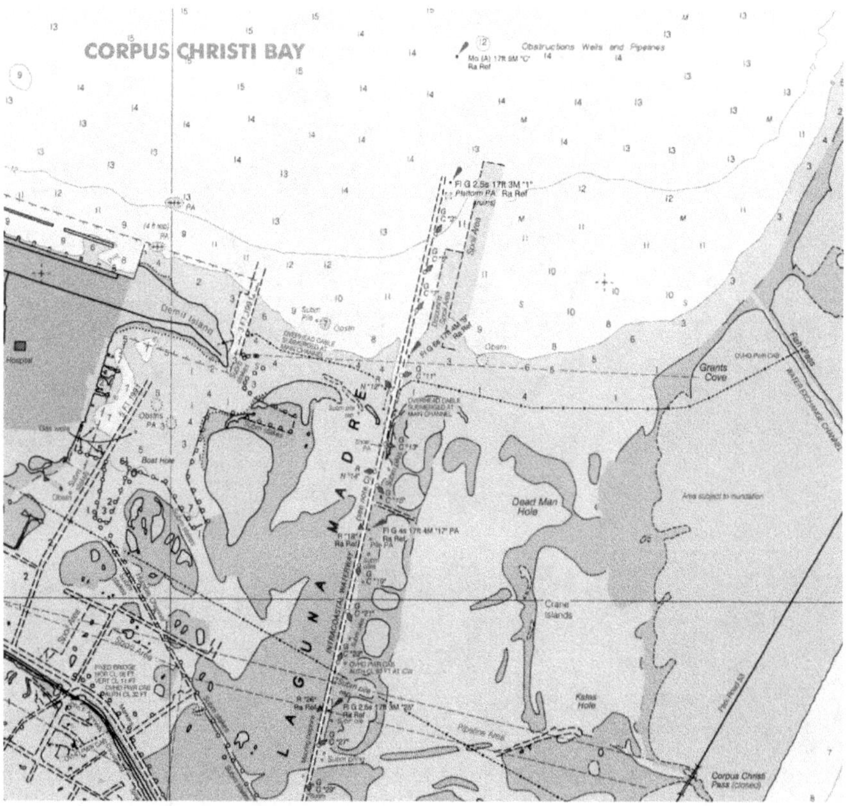

Upper Laguna Madre, as it joins Corpus Christi Bay

Upper Laguna Madre is a good place to seize mixed stringers of trout and redfish.

lays. When the tide is low and the sides are dry, work the cuts leading into the Intracoastal. If the tide is in, expect to see tailing reds on the edge of the grass, even during the heat of the day. Stick to spoons, big topwaters, or a Bass Assassin rigged with only a hook for best results.

Another good method is to drift the shoreline and fish a live shrimp either free-lined or under an Alameda Rattling Float or a Mansfield Mauler rig. This method is especially good when the water is super clear.

PORT O'CONNOR & ESPIRITU SANTO

One of the best places to intercept redfish in Texas is around the gas wells in Espiritu Santo Bay and in the Port O'Connor surf. There are about 20 gas wells in Espiritu. The best way to fish them is to target the shell pads at the

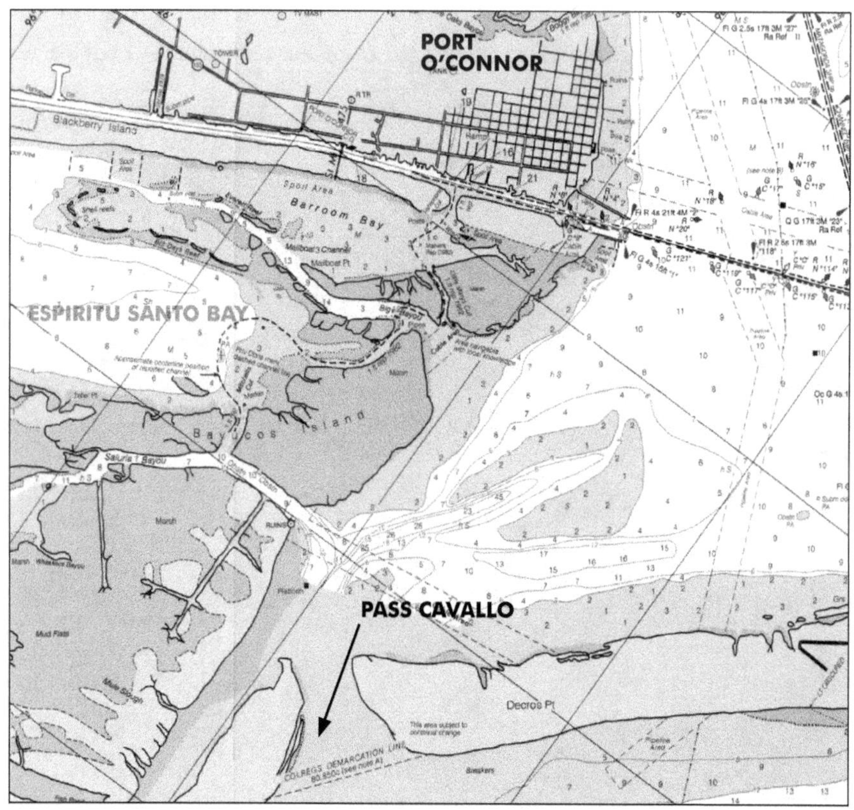

Port O'Connor and Espiritu Santo Bay

bottom. Bouncing a soft plastic will often draw a strike, but fishing with live croaker can be unbelievable. Croaker fishing is very consistent here. Because of their reliability, the gas wells are a good backup plan when you want to go exploring.

Another viable option is running the surf out of Pass Cavalo. When light southeast winds blow, the fishing is tough to beat. Much of this has to do with structure along the beach. The only structure on most beaches is sand and more sand. In this area, there are a number of shrimp boat wrecks that always hold some very large fish in summer. Throwing live croaker around those wrecks is good as is a gold spoon or MirrOlure.

HANNA'S REEF (GALVESTON BAY)

As noted, Upper Coast hotspots go, Hanna's Reef in Galveston Bay is one of the best known. The entire area from the reef to near Lady's Pass

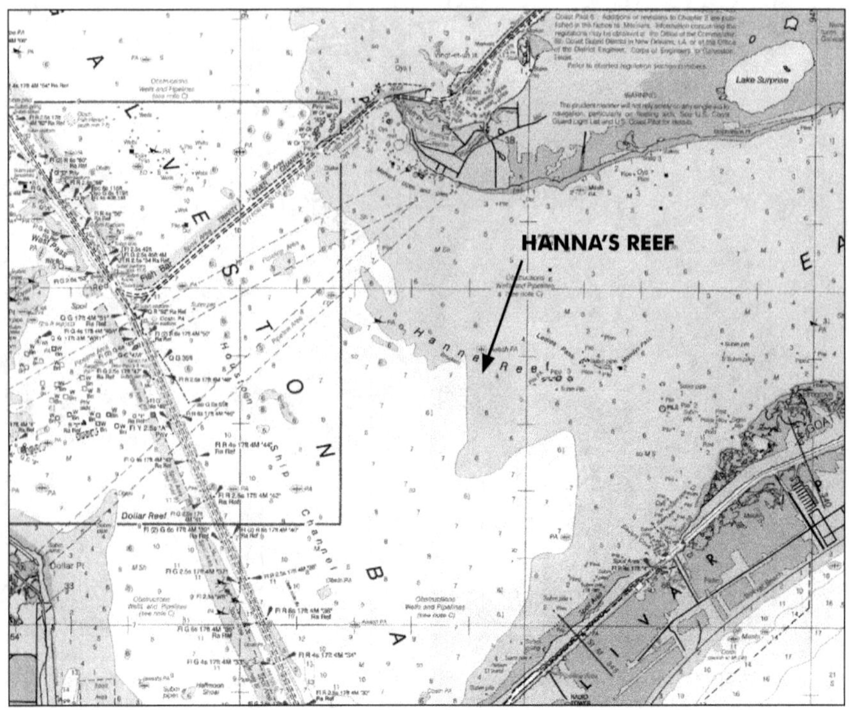

Hanna's Reef on Galveston Bay

and Bull Hill has been a consistent producer of redfish, particularly during the spring and early summer. This area is especially productive when a light wind coincides with a low, incoming tide. These conditions are ideal, but as long as the tide is moving, the reds will bite.

The 51 Series MirrOlures and soft plastics are great to fish over the shell. Someone chucking from a boat might want to go with the 52 Series. Either way, some of the better color patterns are chartreuse, pink, and white with gold sides, Bass Assassins also work great here. Shell reefs are often loaded with sand eels, which reds love. As such, a soft plastic jerkbait makes a good sand eel imitation.

SOUTH JETTY (PORT ARANSAS)

During summer months, jetties give anglers some of the most consistent action for reds. The South Jetty at Port Aransas may be one of the best (even though it's greatly overlooked) in the Texas Coastal Bend. Pre-dawn runs can

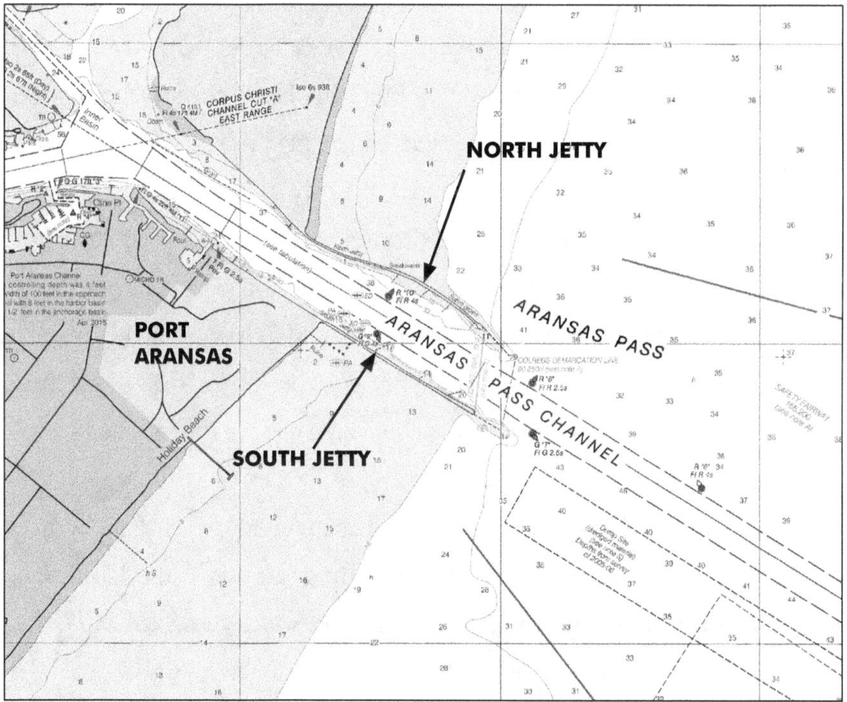

Port Aransas South Jetty

yield good fish on black topwater plugs fished right along the rocks, while later in the day the action shifts to live bait.

Croaker is popular with locals, but piggy perch can be just as effective. My best advice would be to fish as close to the rocks as possible since they hold the fish. Look for little holes in the rocks where water can trade from the Gulf to ship channel side. These spots are magnets to reds. Throw your piggy perch in there and be ready.

PORT MANSFIELD

Anglers looking to get in on some shallow water wade-fishing have plenty of options at Port Mansfield. Gladys Hole just east of the famous Land Cut is a top wade-fishing destination, although it has a soft bottom. Anglers that area really out of shape might want to pass this one by and let the fitness nuts go at it.

The large sandbar east of Marker 110 gives up its share of redfish, as does Butcher's Island near Marker 113. Butcher's Island the top site to get in on tailing redfish action, and on weekends can be highly pressured. It would be a good idea to get there early during times of heavy boat traffic.

Other good spots include the shorelines near markers 17 and 20 and the East Side of Green Island. This spot can be super for reds, but is very, very shallow and can be treacherous for boaters not used to navigating the area. It is also a good place to get stuck when the tide goes out. If you plan to fish here, pay special attention to the tide tables, else, you could wind up waiting for the tide to come back in.

Port Mansfield is on the shores of Laguna Madre, a shallow body of water along the Intracoastal Canal between the coast and Padre Island. The town is 25 miles from Raymondville on Hwy. 186, which runs into US 77. This is a beautiful stretch of highway to drive, especially for those who like to view wildlife.

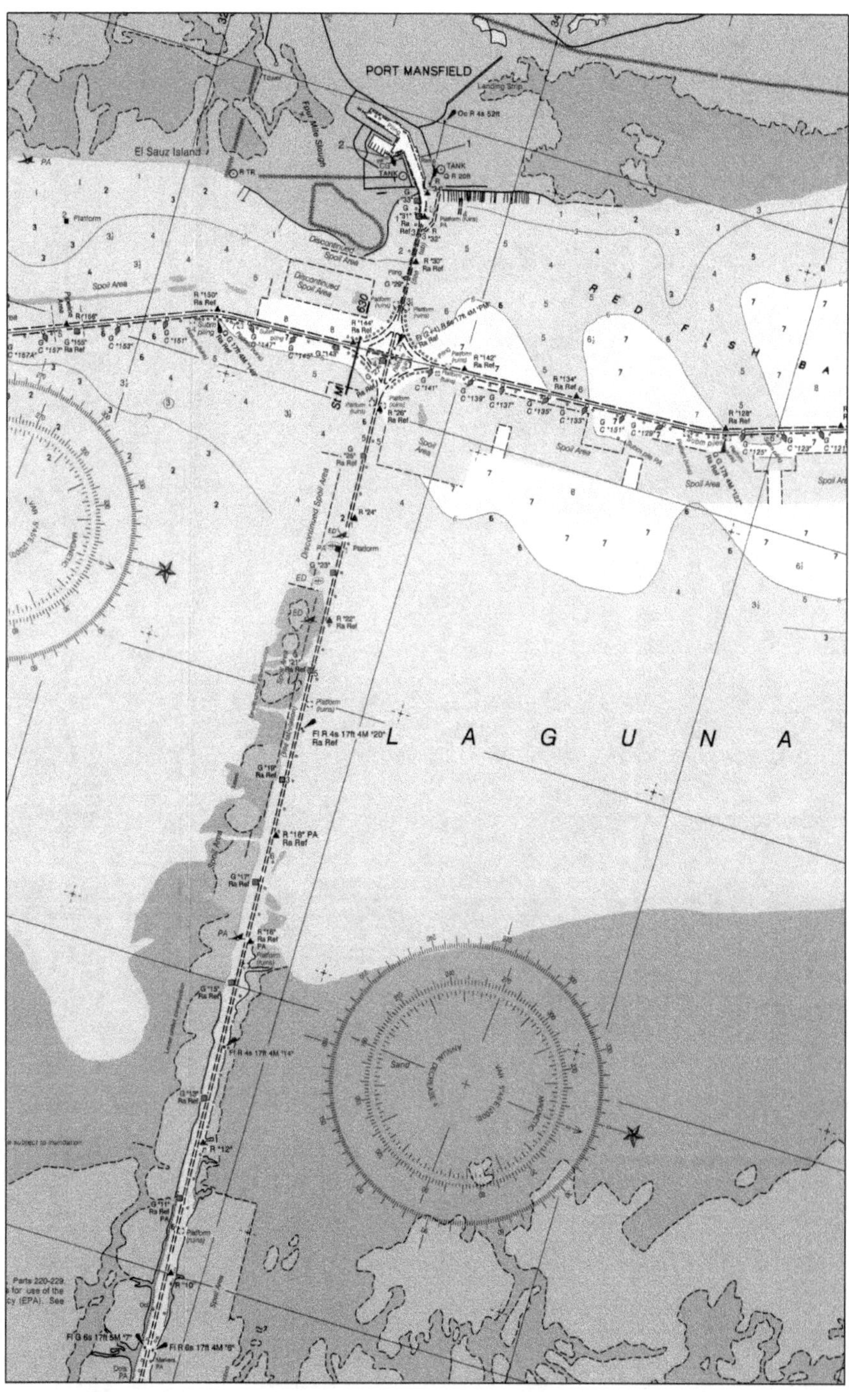

Port Mansfield

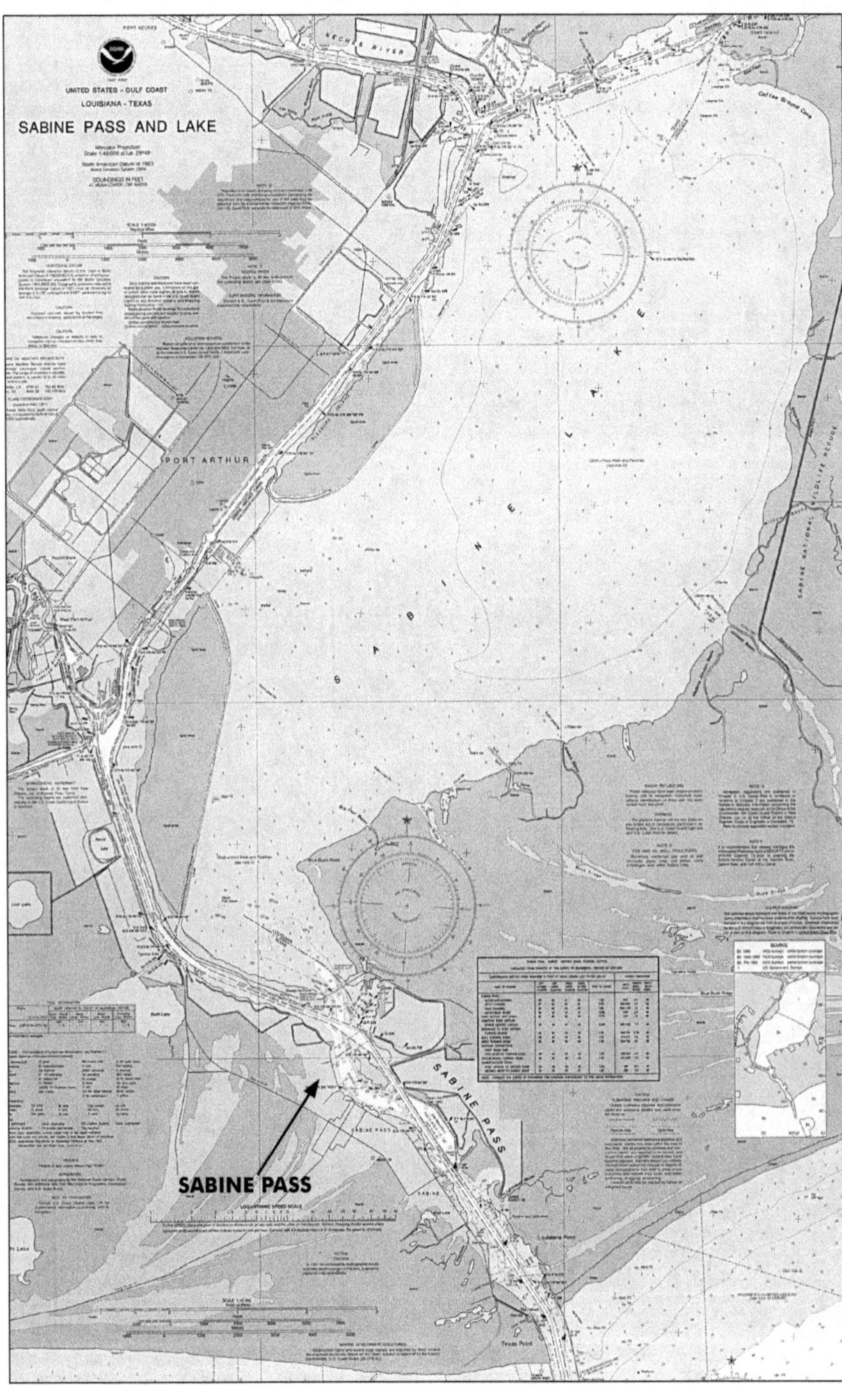

Sabine Lake and Pass

SABINE LAKE

Sabine redfish start their most consistent bite pattern in summer months, which reaches a dramatic climax in the fall. Summer reds school in the open water of bay systems in mid-day "slick offs." Running the open bay looking for hints of bronze on the water and massive schooling action is the best way to locate these brutes. In the nearshore Gulf of Mexico out of Sabine Pass, big schools of reds chase menhaden and shrimp, most frequently between 200 yards and 2 miles from the beach front.

Gold spoons and Rat-L-Traps are best for schooling reds in the bays, while the ones offshore turn up their noses to anything except live or fresh-cut fish and crab. During the early part of fall, the attention turns back to the shorelines. Anglers wading or fishing with carpeted flat bottom boats or skiffs should look for tailing reds or fish cruising along shorelines.

Winter months see redfish action dwindling to near nothing. About the only consistent action is at the Entergy Plant warm water discharge. Bull redfish still haunt the Sabine Jetties.

KEITH LAKE

Keith Lake is the first of a long series of small lakes that border the town of Sabine Pass, Texas. The area has many sloughs, cuts, and marshy shorelines

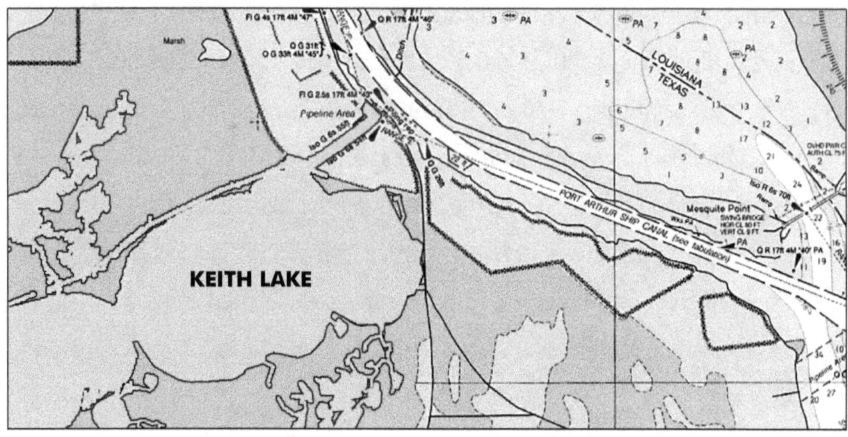

Keith Lake

to fish. One of the best spots is where Keith Lake Cut empties into the lake. There is a spot where sand meets a mud bottom and schools often congregate there.

LAKE CALCASIEU

This Louisiana hotspot is best known for its monster speckled trout, but the redfish action is even better. During spring when the redfish action starts, anglers here have serious problems with the wind.

"If the wind blows hard, it's difficult to fish a lot of the open areas, which puts a damper on the trout fishing. That is why a lot of people are op to chase reds in the marsh now," said Ken Chaumont longtime fishing industry insider and lure developer.

Anglers with carpeted flat bottom boats or skiffs should look for tailing reds or fish cruising along shorelines. A way to increase the odds of seeing these fish is to wear polarized sunglasses, which takes the glare off the water and allows you to see into the water much better.

Capt. Erik Rue said there are plenty other great spots for red in Lake Calcasieu: "There are lots of great places during later summer and early fall. Turney's Bay gets good going into fall and can be good in summer as well, although the pattern is live bait. The good thing about summer is the lack of wind, which helps the water clarity in that area. We have such a muddy bottom in a very shallow lake that it does not take much of a wind to stir it up. Turney's Bay is best on a light wind out of the north or the west with an outgoing tide."

Commissary Point is one of the areas I fished with Chaumont a couple of years ago. It is in the middle of the lake along the eastern shoreline just south of Hebert's Landing. Rue said of it: "Commissary Point is a good spot to hit after most of the boats have left and the water clears. The key here is bait. It's deeper than much of the lake and always has a steady bait supply and good numbers of fish."

Rue said anglers looking for big fish should hit Lambert's Bayou, Lambert's Bayou Reef, or Grand Bayou: "Those are good spots to catch big fish

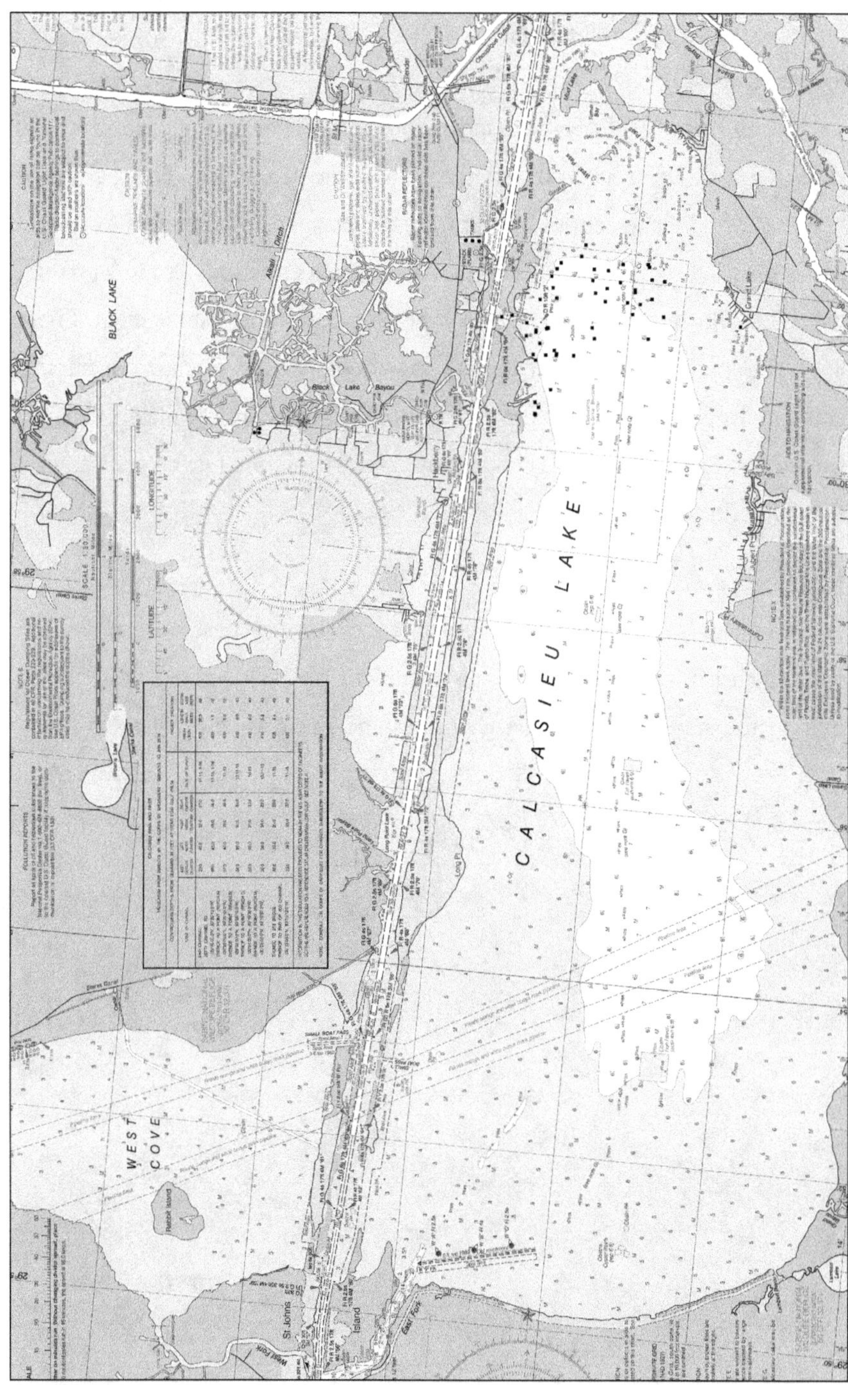

Lake Calcasiue, Louisiana

on live bait, or to throw topwaters. Lots of huge fish have been caught there in recent years."

One of my Dad's favorite spots from yesteryear that still produces today is the old rock jetties along the southern shoreline of the lake. The rocks there hold lots of baitfishes, shrimp, and plenty of hefty reds. Rue prefers to fish the jetties on a light incoming tide, and looks for concentrations of mullet to find fish. The Old Jetties are also a great spot for anglers to fish at night. Green lights set up along the rocks can draw in incredible concentrations of baitfish, and therefore equally impressive numbers of reds. Live shrimp is a good choice for night fishing, but soft plastics in glow, chartreuse, or white colors also yield strong catches.

CONSTANCE BEACH

Located just south of Lake Calcasieu, Constance Beach offers some of the best surf fishing for reds in Louisiana. Many big bulls run this beach beginning in the summer, with peak action around the middle of October. What

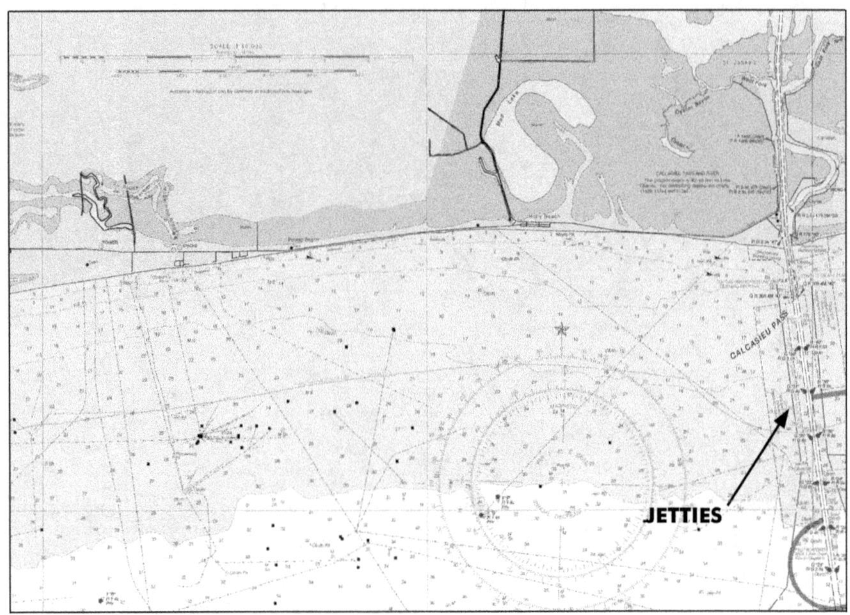

Constance Beach, Louisiana

makes Constance Beach so great is the system of rock jetties. The rocks hold many crab, and in turn lots of redfish. Anglers wanting to catch the Big One should fish with crab, cut mullet, or croaker out past the rocks. For anglers wanting to tangle with big reds on lighter gear, chunk DOA Shrimp or gold spoons along the rocks. This, by the way, is Capt. Terry Shaunessy's favorite spot to catch bull redfish.

VENICE

The marshes in Venice, La. offer the only reliable sight casting to 40 plus inch redfish I am aware of anywhere. I caught my biggest ever red, a 46-incher

Marshes of the Mississippi River Delta, south of Venice, Louisiana

in 18 inches of water there fishing a huge soft plastic swim bait under a popping cork. This area is a virtual maze of canals and shallow flats that can get an angler in trouble so hiring a guide there is definitely recommended.

CHANDELEUR ISLANDS

These barrier islands located off the coasts of Louisiana and Mississippi are known widely for their phenomenal speckled trout fishing, but they are loaded with redfish. Any of the islands can hold reds, but the shallow coves of

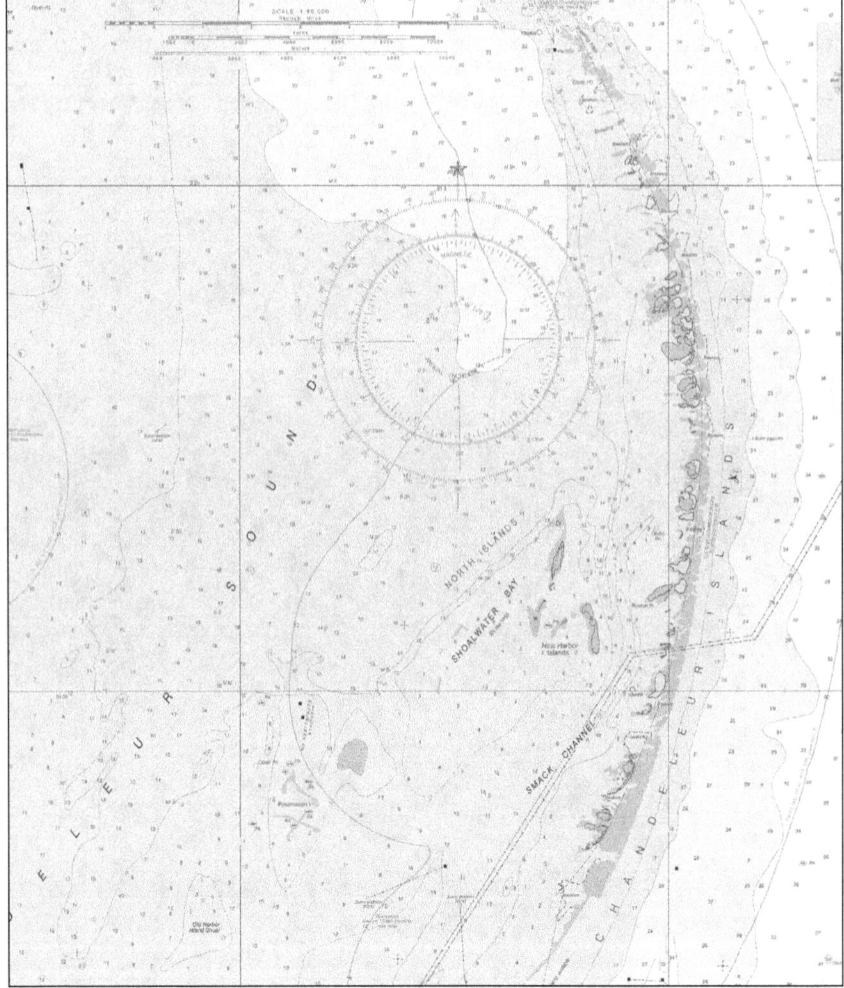

Chandeleur Islands

Breton Island and the surf side of the big islands near Biloxi holds lots of them. Give the nearby oil rigs a try. They are loaded with big bulls.

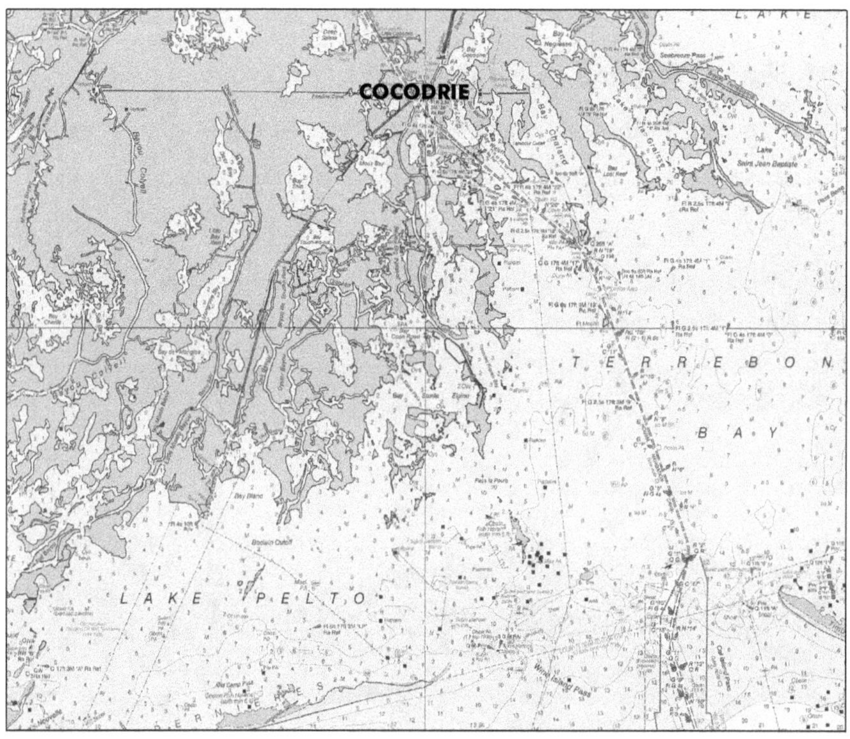

Cocodrie, Louisiana

COCODRIE, LOUISIANA

The marshes of Cocodrie in southern Louisiana are some of the most fertile in the world and, boy, do they produce reds. Fly-fishermen flock to the area to seek tailing reds in the shallow flats and cuts.

BANK-FISHING HOTSPOTS

Having to fish from the bank is not an enviable task. Most of the best fishing spots are not accessible to bank-fishermen, and those that can be reached from land are often crowded. Nonetheless, land-bound anglers in Texas have it better than folks in other areas. We have plentiful access to good bank-fishing, especially in saltwater. Some areas are well known and can be highly pressured at times, while others see little pressure. The following are some of the best bank-fishing spots on the coast.

PLEASURE ISLAND

Located on the west bank of Sabine Lake, Pleasure Island offers miles of access to bank-fishing. One of the best spots is at the causeway bridge at the Texas/Louisiana border on Highway 82. The area around the bridge is excellent during spring and fall. Less than 100 yards from the bridge is the Walter Umphrey Pier, a free, lighted fishing pier.

PHOTO: WIKIMEDIA COMMONS

Pleasure Island, Port Arthur, Texas

The other popular fishing areas here are the north and south revetment walls. A public road runs alongside the walls. Anglers can fish either from the rocks or from one of several small, free fishing piers that dot the wall. Anglers can also fish and crab in the revetment ponds themselves. They are great spots to catch redfish.

To get to Pleasure Island take the Highway 73 in Port Arthur to the Highway 82 (Martin Luther King) Exit. Follow 82 over the Martin Luther King Bridge and you are on Pleasure Island.

TEXAS BAYOU

Texas Bayou, located in Sabine Pass, feeds into the Sabine-Neches ship channel about one mile north of the jetties. A bridge and dock provide good

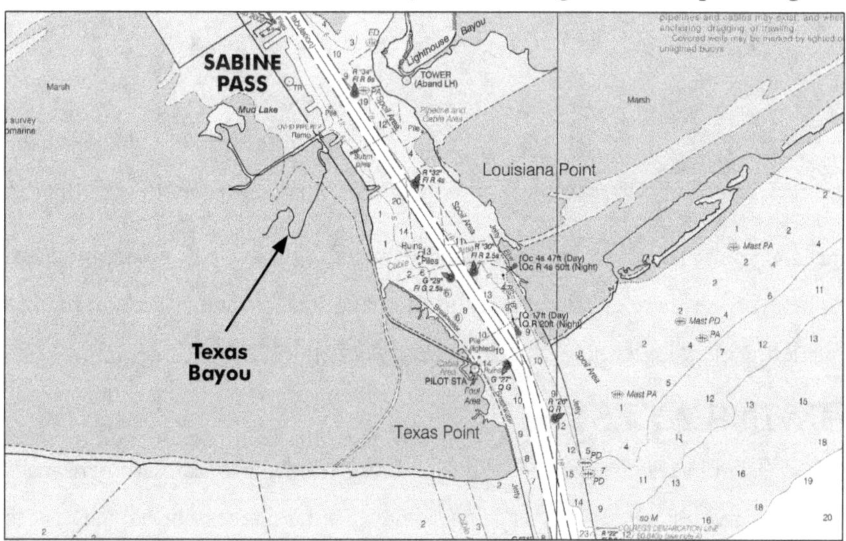

Texas Bayou

fishing for reds. Crabbing is also good here. To get to Texas Bayou take Highway 87 to Sabine Pass. When you get there, go straight at the four-way and follow the curving road to the left. About 1/4 mile down the road, you will see a stop sign. From there take a right and follow the road for a mile until you reach a small bridge. That's Texas Bayou.

DICK DOWLING PARK

Years ago, Dick Dowling Park used to be popular a popular redfish spot. Fewer anglers fish there now, but the fishing can still be good. If you decided to fish here, bring a rod that can cast a long way. There are many hang-ups just

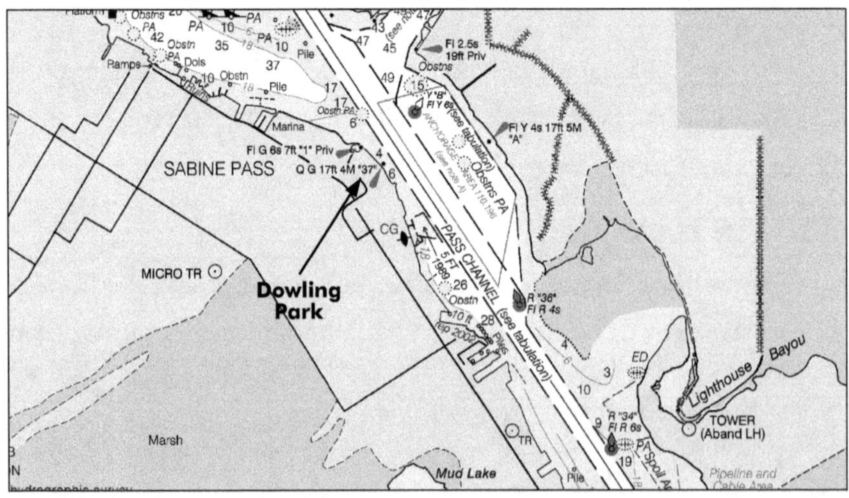

Dick Dowling Park

off the bank. To get to Dick Dowling Park, take Highway 87 to Sabine Pass. When you get there, go straight at the four-way and follow the curving road to the left. You will see the park signs a on the left side.

TWIN LAKES

Twin Lakes just outside of Bridge City has been popular with bank-fishermen for years. The fishing is good because of the diversity of habitat. There is a deep canal on one side and shallow marsh on the other. This is where I cut my teeth fishing by catching redfish, black drum, flounder, and garfish.

Some of the best spots include the deeper water around the bridge and along the saltwater barrier. Most of the fishing is on the side of the road where the power plant is located. The lake on the opposite side of the road is fishable, but it is extremely shallow. There are two culverts here, which allow water to exchange from both sides of the highway. These are good spots to crab and

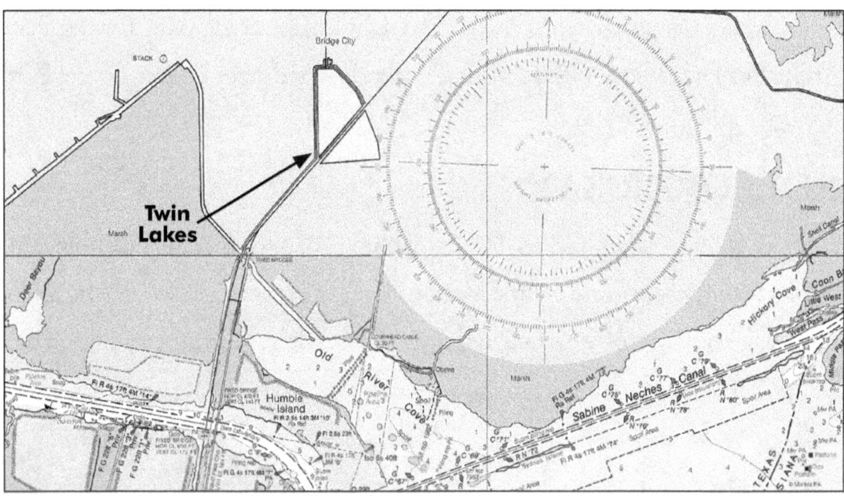

Twin Lakes

catch live bait. The Twin Lakes are located between Bridge City and Port Arthur on Highway 87.

LAKE ROAD

More commonly known as "Bailey Road" because the Bailey family has operated a bait camp there for years, the Lake Road area offers good fishing. The area near Bailey's Bait Camp allows access to wadefish Sabine Lake in Old River Cove, which is one of my old standbys for reds.

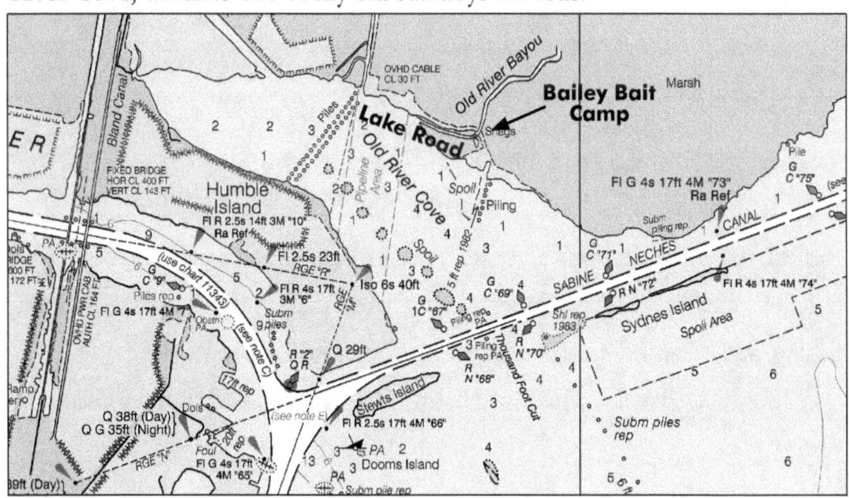

Lake (Bailey) Road

Lake Road is located at the last red light leaving Bridge City toward Port Arthur on Highway 87. That would be the first red light coming from Port Arthur.

ROLLOVER BAY

Rollover Pass pass has been blocked, but it was once one of the most popular bank-fishing destinations on the Upper Coast. That is because anglers could fish along both sides of the pass and waders had easy access to prime wading on the

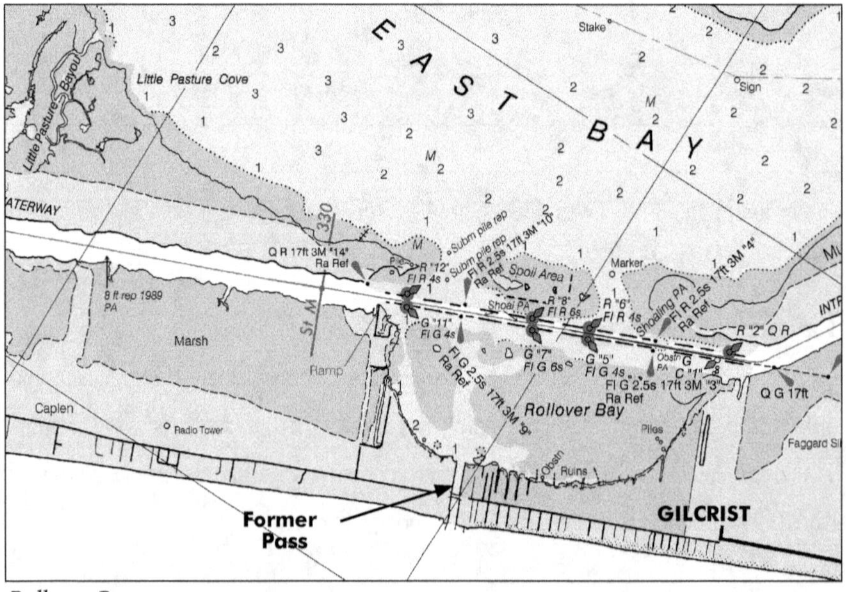

Rollover Bay

flats near the channel on the north end. Those flats are still productive.

The best bait for reds is something live. Live shrimp fall easily to bait stealers, so mud minnows, shad, and croaker are better choices. Mud minnows are the standard issue in these parts due to the excellent flounder fishing, and will more than suffice for the other popular game fish.

Rollover Bay is located on Highway 87 between Gilcrist and Galveston.

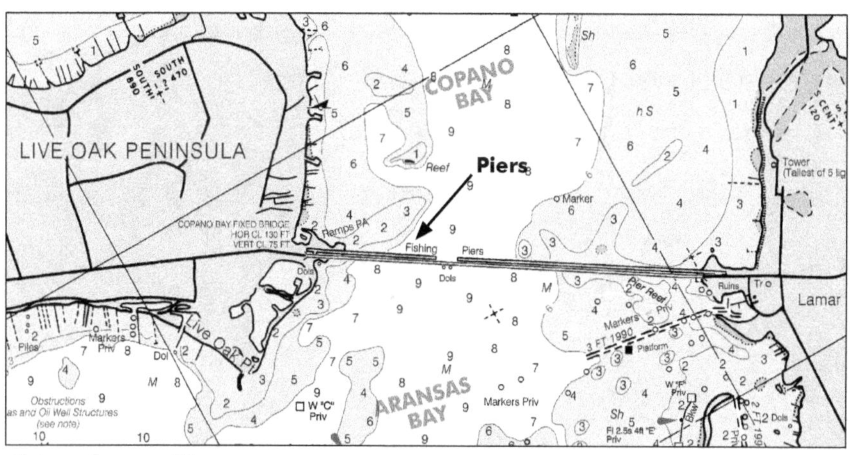

Copano Causeway Pier

COPANO CAUSEWAY PIER (ARANSAS BAY)

Located on Highway 35 N, the pier divides Copano Bay and Aransas Bay. It is lighted, has cleaning tables, and is open seven days a week, 24 hours a day. Contact the north end at 361-729-8519, the south end at 361-729-7762.

ARANSAS NATIONAL WILDLIFE REFUGE

Located along San Antonio and Aransas Bays, the 70,504 acres of the Aransas National Wildlife Refuge is well known for its resident wildlife and

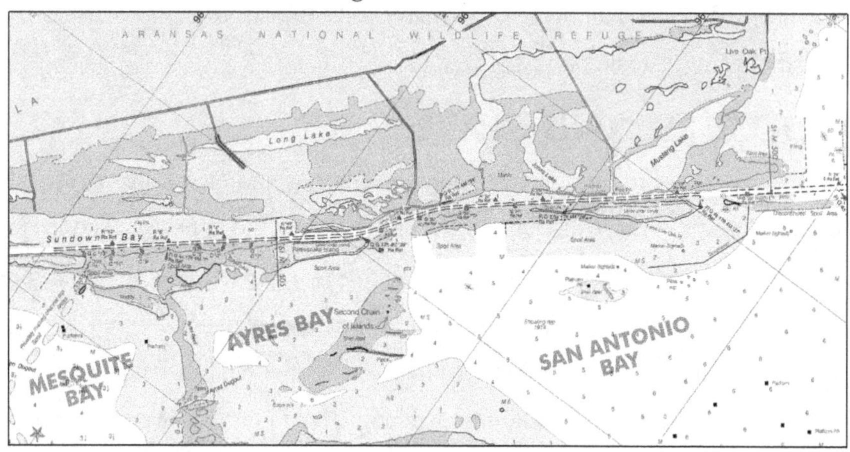

Aransas National Wildlife Refuge

winter whooping cranes. There are some fine fishing opportunities to be found there, too. For more information, call 512-286-3559.

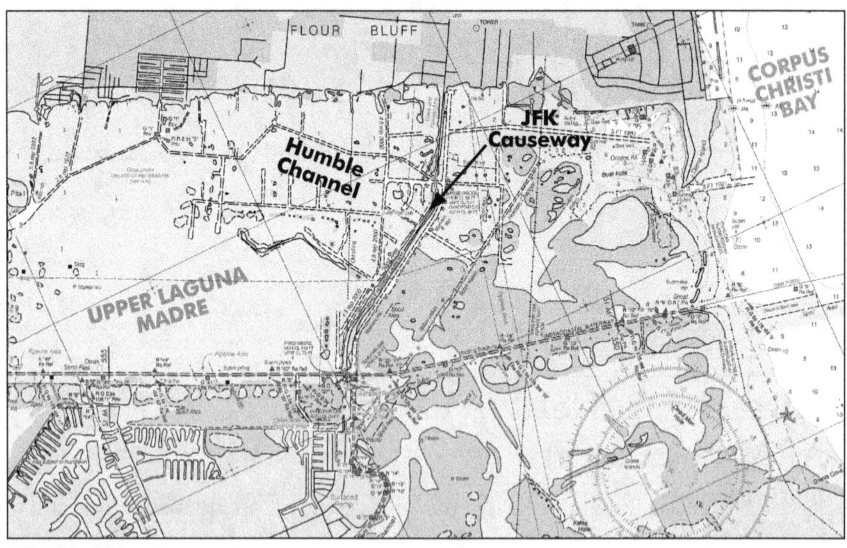

Humble Channel

HUMBLE CHANNEL AT THE JFK CAUSEWAY (CORPUS CHRISTI)

Located between Baffin Bay and Port Aransas, this area is a favorite of experienced bank-fishermen. There are two piers, one at Trainer's Marina, another at Red Dot Bait Stand. This is an excellent place to catch redfish, particularly during the fall months.

GOOSE ISLAND STATE PARK

This 321-acre park is surrounded by Aransas and St. Charles Bays and offers anglers a good chance at redfish. The shoreline is comprised of concrete bulkhead, oyster shell, mud, flat and marsh grass. Anglers fishing along the concrete bulkhead with cane poles and live shrimp occasionally pull up big reds. Most anglers fish with crab or mullet out in the bay. Facilities include a fish cleaning shelter and a 1,620-foot lighted pier with two fish-cleaning tables. For more information, call 361-729-2858.

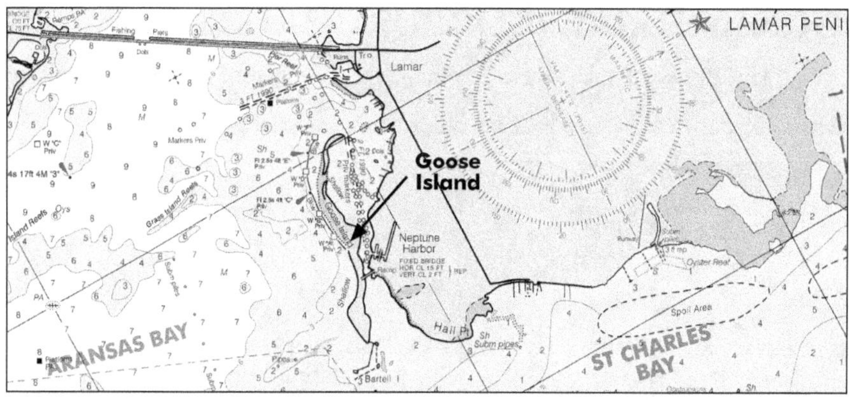

Goose Island State Park

MATAGORDA ISLAND STATE PARK (PORT O'CONNOR)

If seclusion if your idea of a good time, then this is your spot. This is one of the best spots in the state to catch bull redfish in the late summer and fall.

The surf here gets deep quick, so be careful when wading out to cast a surf rod, and be especially careful at night—when the big sharks will be prowling. More than likely, they will not attack you, but if you smell like menhaden or bloody mullet, there is no telling what might happen. Use your head because Matagorda Island is a long way from a hospital. For more information, call 361-983-2215.

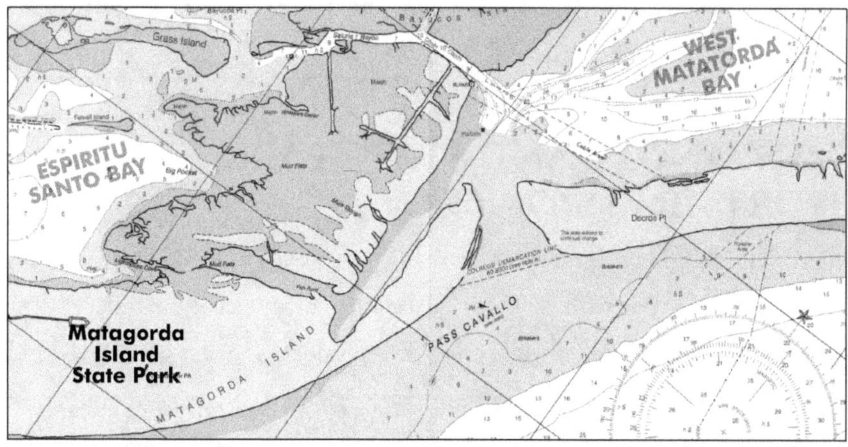

Matagorda Island State Park

OCEAN DRIVE (CORPUS CHRISTI)

This drive will take you along the main shoreline of Corpus Christi Bay near Cole Park Pier, Oso Pier, and other bank- and wade-fishing locations.

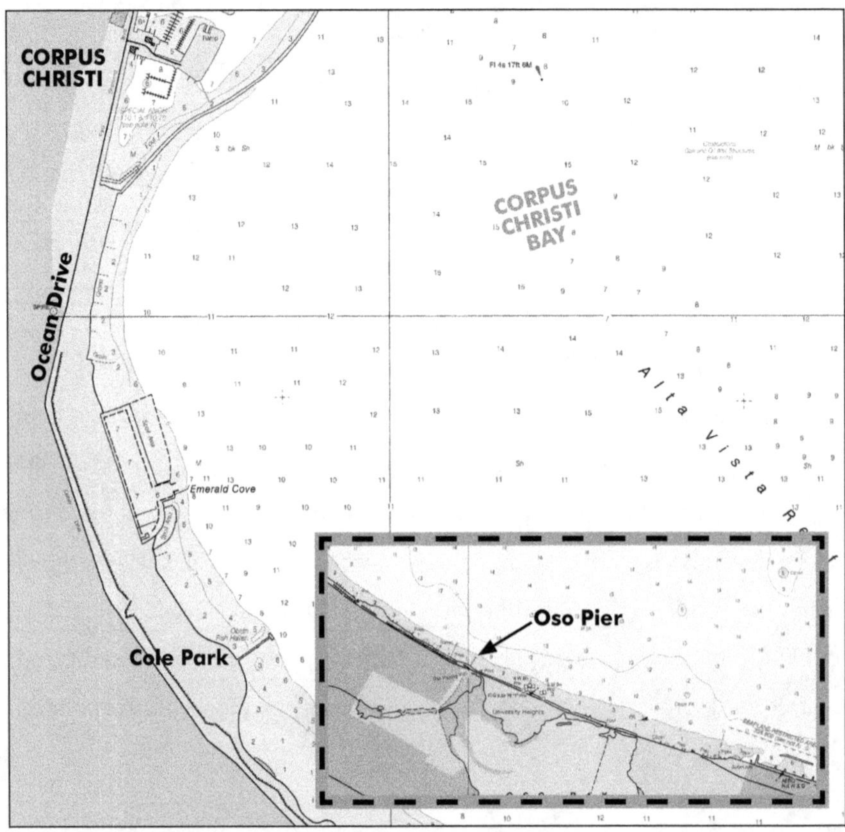

Ocean Drive in Corpus Christi

MUSTANG ISLAND STATE PARK (PORT ARANSAS)

This 3,954-acre park offers five miles of beach on the Gulf of Mexico, and it is loaded with redfish. This is a secluded, unique ecosystem dependent upon sand dunes. Coastal dunes are the product of wind-deposited sand anchored by sparse mats of vegetation. The height of well-vegetated dunes may reach 35 feet in some areas of the park. If you plan on doing much walking, be

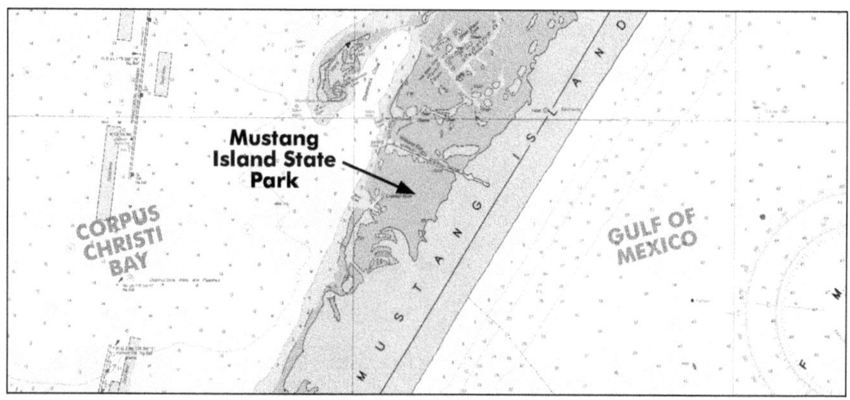

Mustang Island State Park

prepared to contend with the dunes. If you plan on driving down the beach, be careful not to get stuck. The sand here is infamous for that. For more information, call 512-389-8900.

PADRE ISLAND NATIONAL SEASHORE

This is Texas' single largest bank-fishing spot. Counting both sides of the island, there are more than 150 miles of fishing holes covering the Gulf of Mexico and Laguna Madre. It offers the bulk of South Texas bank-fishing.

According to U.S. Fish and Wildlife Service officials, Padre Island National Seashore encompasses 133,000 acres of America's vanishing barrier

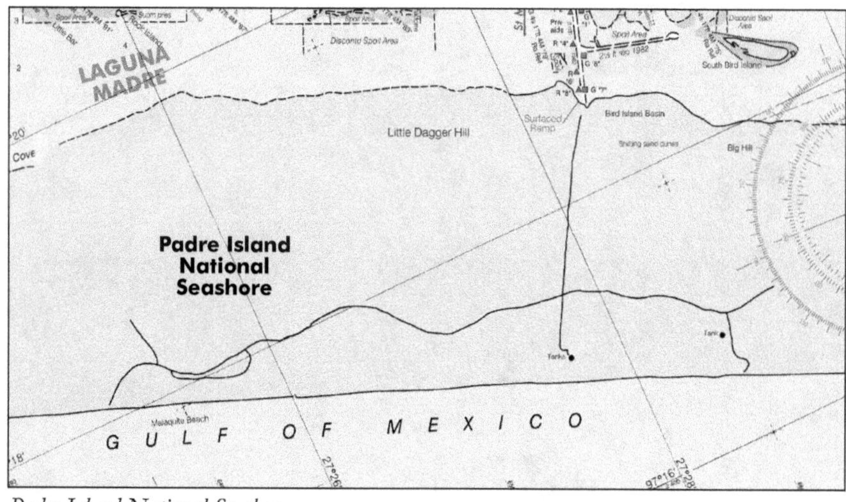

Padre Island National Seashore

islands. It is the longest remaining undeveloped barrier island in the world. Part of Padre Island's greatness as a fishing destination comes from its diversity. Waders can venture chest-deep into the blue-green waters and chuck surface lures for slot-sized reds, while their counterparts battle big bull sharks on surf rods from the white sand beaches.

The biggest problem with Padre Island is its remoteness. There is a whole lot of island that sees very few people due to the inhospitable nature of the sand dunes. Some of the easier places to reach are Malaquite Beach, a semi-primitive campground with water, restrooms, showers and a concession stand with plenty of excellent fishing holes. There is also Bird Island Basin, which offers great fishing and a very primitive campsite with only pit toilets.

WILLACY COUNTY PARK PIER (PORT MANSFIELD)

This 500-foot lighted pier offers good access to Laguna Madre and routinely produces good catches of reds in the summer and spring months. Besides

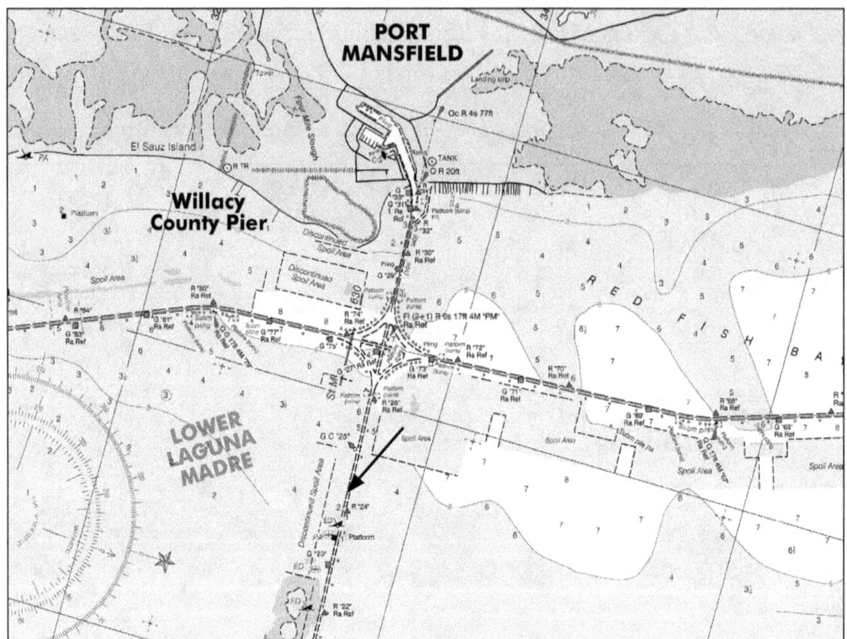

Willacy County Park Pier

the pier, there are also picnic tables, barbecue pits, and restrooms. For more information, call 956-944-4000.

CAMERON COUNTY PARKS (HARLINGEN)

The Cameron County Park System leases property from the Laguna Atascosa National Wildlife Refuge along the Arroyo Colorado River. Adolph

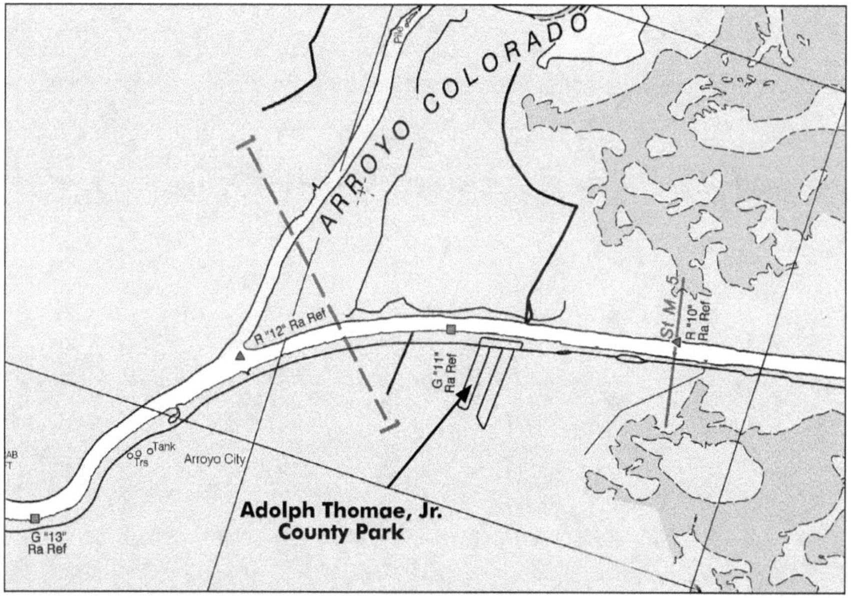

Adolph Thomae, Jr. County Park on the Arroyo Colorado

Thomae, Jr. County Park provides fishing piers and a boat launch along with RV and campsites. The fishing here ranges from fair to good for redfish. For more information, call 956-748-2044.

BOCA CHICA STATE PARK (PORT ISABEL)

Boca Chica State Park is just under 1,100 acres, located in the Boca Chica Sub delta of the Rio Grande River, in southeastern Cameron County. The south shore of South Bay, west shore of Boca Chica Bay, and the flat, sandy, northern end of Boca Chica Island are prime redfish spots. The water is generally very

Boca Chica State Park

clear, so adjust fishing tactics accordingly and look for drop-offs from the shallow water. Most of the aquatic terrain here is flat, and even the slightest depth change will hold fish. For more information, call 956-585-1107.

Chapter Twelve

Redfish Recipes

Redfish are tops in the frying pan, on the grill or in the oven. Their flesh has a mild taste and texture, and they yield a lot of meat per pound of fish. The following recipes are some I have tried over the years, some from anglers in Texas, Louisiana, and Florida. They range from simple to quite elaborate.

Enjoy.

REDFISH ON THE HALF SHELL

1 fresh redfish

onion powder, garlic powder, salt, pepper

1 12-oz beer, strong

1/4 stick butter

1 Tbs. Worcestershire

1 clove garlic, crushed

1 tsp Caribbean jerk seasoning

Fillet the fish leaving the skin and scales on. Lay the fillet skin side down. Sprinkle flesh side with onion power, fresh garlic, salt, and pepper, and rub in with your fingers. Put the fish in the fridge for one to two hours to marinate. Make the following sauce just before taking the fish out of the fridge.

In a medium saucepan, combine beer, butter, Worcestershire sauce, garlic, jerk seasoning, and a little pepper. Stir ingredients over a medium flame until blended and butter is melted. Oil the skin side of the redfish and then place the fish skin side down on a hot grill. Baste the flesh with the sauce every 10 minutes. Cook the fish 30 to 45 minutes over low to medium heat. The skin will curl up, keeping the sauce on the meat and making it very moist. Fish flakes easily when done. Remove fish from the grill; most of the scales will stay on the grill.

BLACKENED REDFISH

6 8- to 10-oz. fish fillets, 1/2 to 3/4 inches thick
1/2 lb. unsalted butter, melted
1/2 Tbs. paprika
2 1/2 tsp. salt
1 tsp. onion powder
1 tsp. garlic powder
1 tsp. ground red pepper
3/4 tsp. white pepper
1/2 tsp. black pepper
1/2 tsp. dried thyme
1/2 tsp. dried oregano

Combine seasonings. (A prepared blackened seasoning may be substituted.) Cook outdoors as it creates copious smoke.

Heat a large cast iron skillet over high heat. Dip each fillet in butter and coat with seasoning mix. Place in hot skillet and top with one tsp. butter. Cook uncovered over high heat about two minutes. Turn and cook two more minutes, serve immediately.

ROYAL REDFISH

4 redfish, skinned and filleted (5 pounds)
1/2 cup oil
1/2 cup flour
2 med. onions, chopped
1 clove garlic, minced
1/2 cup celery, chopped
1/2 cup green pepper, chopped
1 8-oz. can tomato sauce
1 14-1/2-oz. can tomatoes
1/4 cup parsley, chopped
1 bay leaf
1/2 tsp. allspice
pinch of basil
2 sprigs saffron
1 cup water
1 cup red wine (Burgundy)
salt and pepper, to taste
lemon juice

Make a medium-dark roux with oil and flour in a large skillet (cast iron is best). Add onion, green pepper, celery, and garlic to roux and sauté until tender. Add tomato sauce, tomatoes, parsley, rest of seasonings, salt, and pepper to taste. Simmer slowly for 35 minutes. (At this point, you may freeze for later use.) Add water slowly and cook down to thick gravy. Add wine and more water (if needed) to make sauce medium thick. Rub fish with lemon, salt and pepper lightly, and then place in large baking dish. Pour sauce over fish and bake 40 to 50 minutes or until flaky in preheated 350 oven.

REDFISH BEIGNETS

3 pounds redfish
hot sauce
3 cups flour
1 cup cornstarch
1 Tbs. paprika
1 tsp. cayenne pepper
2 Tbs. salt
1/2 tsp. garlic powder

Marinate redfish in hot sauce for 1 hour or more. Combine remaining ingredients to make breading. Roll redfish in breading and deep fry at 350 until fish pieces float. Remove from deep fry and place on a paper towel.

Make a sauce by combining:

1 cup mayonnaise
1/4 cup sour cream
1 Tbs. Dijon mustard
salt and pepper to taste

Place a leaf lettuce on a salad plate. Spoon beignet sauce onto lettuce. Place redfish beignets on plate. Garnish with a carrot curl and chopped parsley, and serve.

SAUSAGE CRUSTED REDFISH WITH SHOESTRING POTATOES

6 Tbs. olive oil

2 zucchini, sliced lengthwise into 1-inch thick slices

2 yellow squash, sliced lengthwise into 1-inch thick slices

2 eggplant, sliced lengthwise into 1-inch thick slices

1 cup roasted pecan pieces

2 tsp. garlic, chopped

1/4 cup green onions, chopped

3/4 cup Worcestershire sauce

2 med lemons, skin and pith removed

2 bay leaves

3/4 cup cold butter, cubed

3 oz. smoked sausage, finely diced

1 cup breadcrumbs

1 Tbs. Cajun seasoning

4 6- to 8-oz. redfish fillets

2 cups shoestring potatoes

chives

Parmesan cheese

salt and pepper to taste

Preheat oven to 450. Season the vegetables with two Tbs. olive oil, salt, and pepper. Place in a roasting pan and roast for 10 minutes. Remove from oven and cool. Dice and set aside.

In a large sauté pan, cook roasted vegetables, pecans, and garlic in 1 Tbs. Olive oil for two minutes, season with salt and pepper. Stir in green onions and keep warm. In a saucepan, combine the Worcestershire sauce, lemons, and bay leaves. Simmer until reduced by 2/3. Whisk in butter cubes one at a time. The sauce should be thick and coat the back of a spoon. Keep warm. In a hot sauté pan, steam the sausage for two minutes with a few Tbs. of water. Remove from heat and cool completely. Turn sausage into a mixing bowl and combine with breadcrumbs.

Season fillets with Cajun seasoning. In a large, oven-proof sauté pan, heat the remaining olive oil. Add redfish, topside down. Sauté four minutes and turn. Cover the top of each fillet with a quarter of the sausage crust. Place sauté pan in oven and cook for minutes.

To assemble, spoon the sauce in the center and around the rim of each plate. Mound the shoestrings in the center of each plate, then place fillet to the side. Garnish with red and yellow peppers, chives, and cheese.

CREOLE REDFISH

6 lbs. redfish fillets
1/4 lb. butter
6 onions, chopped
1 bell pepper
4 sticks celery, chopped
1 cup shallots, chopped
3 whole pickles (any kind)
25 pimento stuffed olives
1/2 cup fresh parsley, chopped
4 cloves garlic, minced
1 cup fresh sliced mushrooms
3 tsp. Worcestershire
1 lemon sliced
juice of two lemons

Melt butter in a large cast iron pot. Sauté onions until brown. Add bell pepper, celery, and shallots, cook until tender. Add remaining ingredients except fish, lemon juice, and lemon slices. Cook 20 minutes. Place redfish in roasting pan and cover with sauce. Sprinkle with lemon juice and garnish with lemon slices. Bake in 350 oven 1-1/2 to 2 hours.

BARBECUED REDFISH

1 5- to 6-lb. redfish, whole cleaned
1 bell pepper, chopped
3 sticks celery, chopped
3 cloves garlic, chopped
1 medium onion, chopped
2 8-oz. bottles Zesty Italian salad dressing
1 cup white wine
2 Tbs. Worcestershire sauce
2 sticks butter or margarine
1/2 can beer
2 Tbs. catsup
salt and pepper to taste

Cook all ingredients except fish about 90 minutes on a low fire in a 2-quart saucepan. Stir occasionally to keep from sticking. Place fish in roasting pan and fill inside with ingredients. Cook on barbecue pit uncovered for 45 minutes to one hour, basting every 15 to 20 minutes. Salt and pepper to taste.

REDFISH CASSEROLE

2 lb. redfish fillets
1/2 cup Creamy Italian salad dressing
1/2 cup butter, melted

1-1/2 cups Potato chips, crumbled

8 slices American cheese

(Note: Do not use ridged potato chips and use only "creamy" dressing.)

Place fish in a 9x12 baking dish. Pour salad dressing and melted butter over fish. Sprinkle with potato chips and add cheese slices. Bake 15 minutes in a preheated 350 oven.

REDFISH WITH BASIL BUTTER

4 6-oz. redfish fillets

1/4 tsp. Paprika

1/2 cup slivered fresh basil

2 Tbs. unsalted butter

2 Tbs. olive oil

2 Tbs. fresh lemon juice

salt and pepper to taste

Preheat broiler. Cover a baking sheet with foil. Melt butter in small saucepan, add olive oil and lemon juice, cook 5 minutes over low heat. Cover and remove pan from heat. Lay fillets on baking sheet and season with a bit of the butter sauce, salt, pepper, and paprika. Broil 4 minutes as close to heat source as possible. Transfer to serving plates and top with remaining lemon butter sauce, sprinkle with fresh basil.

BROILED CHEESY REDFISH

2 lbs. redfish fillets

2 Tbs. lemon juice

1/2 cup Parmesan cheese
1/4 cup butter, softened
3 Tbs. mayonnaise
3 green onions, chopped
1/4 tsp. salt
dash of hot sauce

Place fillets in a single layer on a greased, shallow oven-to-table type broiler pan. Brush with lemon juice. Combine remaining ingredients in a small bowl and set aside. Broil fillets until fish flakes easily when tested with a fork. Remove from oven and spread with cheese mixture. Broil an additional 30 seconds or until cheese is lightly browned and bubbly. Garnish with lemon twists and parsley if desired

CRISPY PECAN REDFISH

1-1/2 lbs. redfish fillets
1 cup milk
2 cup yellow cornmeal
1 tsp. hot sauce
1/2 tsp. salt
1 stick unsalted butter
1/4 cup vegetable oil
1 cup chopped pecans
1 cup chopped parsley
1/2 cup freshly squeezed lemon juice

Wash fillets under cold running water and place in a bowl with milk, hot sauce, and salt. Allow to sit 15 minutes at room temperature. Heat 2 Tbs. butter and vegetable oil in a skillet over medium high heat. Drain fillets and dredge in cornmeal. Fry until crispy and brown, about two minutes on a side; do not crowd the pan. Pour grease out of skillet and add remaining butter. Place over medium heat, add nuts when butter melts. Stir constantly while the nuts brown. Add parsley and lemon juice, stir to combine. Pour sauce over fillets and serve immediately.

PACKET REDFISH

1 lb redfish fillets
2 Tbs. margarine or butter
1/4 cup lemon juice
1 Tbs. chopped parsley
1 tsp. dill weed
1 tsp. salt
1/4 tsp. pepper
1 med. onion, thinly sliced
Paprika

On four large buttered squares of heavy-duty aluminum foil, place equal amounts of fish. In small saucepan, melt margarine, add lemon juice, parsley, dill weed, salt, and pepper. Pour equal amounts over fish. Sprinkle with paprika, top with onion slices. Wrap foil securely around fish, leaving space for fish to expand. Grill or broil 5 to 7 minutes on each side or until fish flakes with fork.

PICKLED REDFISH

2 lbs. redfish fillets
1/2 cup vinegar
4 oz green chili peppers
1 Tbs. orange peel, finely shredded

1/4 cup orange juice

1/4 cup onion, chopped

2 bay leaves

2 cloves garlic, minced

1 orange; thinly sliced

Rinse, seed, and chop green chilies. Place fish fillets in 10-inch skillet, cover with boiling water, simmer covered, 5 to 8 minutes or until fish flakes easily when tested with a fork. Drain, arrange in a shallow dish. Combine vinegar, oil, chili peppers, orange peel, orange juice, onion, bay leaves, garlic, 1 tsp salt, and 1/8 tsp. pepper. Pour over fish. Cover and refrigerate several hours or overnight. Drain off marinade and transfer fish to a serving dish. Serve cold, garnished with orange slices.

REDFISH TACOS

12 Redfish fillets (1-1/2 oz. ea.)

12 corn tortillas

1 cup flour

1 cup beer

garlic powder

pepper

cabbage leaves, chopped medium

1/2 cup mayonnaise

1/2 cup yogurt

salsa

lime wedges

Combine mayonnaise and yogurt, set aside. Mix flour, garlic powder, and pepper. Stir beer into flour mixture until well blended. Wash fish by dipping in cold, lightly salted water. Dry thoroughly and dip in flour batter. Deep fry at 375 until golden brown and crispy.

Heat corn tortillas until soft and hot. On each tortilla, layer fish fillet, mayonnaise mixture, salsa, and cabbage. Top off with squeeze of lime. Fold tortilla over to serve.

SALSA

1 garlic clove, minced
6 tomatoes, peeled, seeded, and diced
1/2 onion, minced
2 Tbs. cilantro leaves, chopped, stems removed
2 jalapeno chilies, seeded and chopped
1-1/2 tsp. salt
1/4 tsp. pepper

Combine ingredients and mix well.

REDFISH SPECIAL

1 lb. redfish fillets
3/4 tsp. seasoned salt
juice of 1 lemon
1/2 pint sour cream
1/4 lb. cheddar cheese

Sprinkle fillets with seasoned salt and lemon juice. Place in broiler pan and broil until fish flakes. Spread with sour cream and sprinkle with grated cheese. Return to oven and broil until cheese melts and cream is bubbly.

REDFISH MARGARITA

4 redfish filets
flour
1/4 cup peanut oil
3 Tbs. butter
1-1/2 oz. tequila
1/2 oz. triple sec
1 Tbs. lime juice
2 Tbs. minced parsley
salt and pepper

Dredge fish in flour and shake off excess. Heat oil in skillet over moderate heat and cook fish 3 to 4 minutes per side or until just done. Remove and keep warm. Discard oil and add butter to pan. When melted, carefully add tequila (it may flame). Add remaining ingredients and cook until the butter foams. Pour over fish and serve.

REDFISH CROQUETTES

2 Tbs. margarine
3 Tbs. cornstarch
3/4 tsp. salt
1/4 tsp. pepper
1 cup milk
3 cups cooked, flaked redfish
1-1/2 Tbs. chopped parsley

1 tsp. lemon juice

1/2 tsp. grated onion

Melt margarine in sauce pan. Blend in cornstarch, salt, and pepper. Remove from heat. Gradually add milk, mixing until smooth. Cook over medium heat, stirring constantly, until mixture thickens and comes to a boil. Boil 1 minute. Stir in remaining ingredients, chill. Shape, roll in dry breadcrumbs, then in slightly beaten egg, then in crumbs again. Pan or deep fry in corn oil until golden brown.

REDFISH PONCHARTRAIN

4 8-oz. redfish fillets

1 cup white crabmeat

1/2 lb. small to medium shrimp, peeled

12 to 14 fresh oysters

6 Tbs. unsalted butter

2 cups seasoned flour

2 Tbs. fresh lemon juice

In a large skillet, melt 4 Tbs. butter over medium-high heat. Dredge fillets in seasoned flour, sauté until golden brown. Remove from skillet to warm platter. Reserve pan juices. Add two tablespoons butter to pan juices, sauté shrimp, crabmeat, and oysters until shrimp turns pink. Add lemon juice, shake pan gently. Top fillets with seafood and serve.

SWEET ONION CRUSTED REDFISH

1 lb. Onion, slivered and fried until crisp

2 cups breadcrumbs

1 Tbs. garlic powder

1 Tbs. onion powder

1 Tbs. minced basil

1 Tbs. minced parsley

1 tsp. salt

1 cup seasoned flour

Toss breadcrumbs, onion, herbs, and spices together in steel bowl. Dredge redfish seasoned flour. Egg wash crust with breadcrumb mixture. Sauté in a large pan over medium heat until done.

SWEET AND SOUR REDFISH

2 lbs. redfish fillets

1 cup flour

1/2 cup cornstarch

2 tsp. baking powder

1 tsp. baking soda

1-1/2 cups cold water (very important that the water is cold, as the batter is very thin)

1 tsp. salt

sweet and sour sauce

Mix batter ingredients and dip dry fish fillets into batter. Let excess drip back into batter bowl. Drop fillets into deep fryer and cook until fish floats or is golden brown. Serve with sweet and sour sauce.

SWEET AND SOUR SAUCE

1-1/2 cup pineapple juice

1 cup sugar

3 Tbs. cornstarch

6 Tbs. vinegar

6 Tbs. catsup

Combine sugar and cornstarch. Blend in vinegar and catsup. Stir in pineapple juice. Cook, stirring, until thickened and clear. Keep sauce warm until needed.

Chapter Thirteen

The Future:
Standing Guard for Redfish

To look at where the future of redfish is heading, it is necessary to first take a brief look at the past. For many years, commercial fishermen targeted redfish heavily with gill nets, purse seines, and other highly effective tools. Fisheries agencies even allowed recreational anglers to use gill nets in Texas to catch reds and other popular fishes. My dad used to run a gill net when he was a kid and talked about catching entire schools of fish at a time. Now it seems like a waste, but back then that was the way people did things.

By the 1970's, the American public fell in love with redfish, partly because of New Orleans Chef Paul Prudhomme's famous "blackened redfish" recipe. The result was that redfish populations were ravaged, and recreational fishermen experienced terrible fishing conditions. A group of concerned coastal anglers fought to get the redfish classified as a game fish and therefore protected from commercial harvest. Many outdoor writers call those days the "redfish wars," which spawned the Gulf Coast Conservation Association (GCCA), now Coastal Conservation Association (CCA).

The banning of commercial redfish harvest along with aggressive stocking efforts spearheaded by the then Gulf Coast Conservation Association (GCCA) and the Texas Parks & Wildlife Department (TPWD) gave the redfish population a much-needed boost. At the time of this writing, Texas has stocked more than 100,000,000 redfish fingerlings into coastal bay systems and estuaries. TPWD officials also placed a slot limit on redfish that protected the mature breeding specimens (bull reds) from harvest.

By the early 1990's, redfish numbers had stabilized and recreational fishermen started catching lots of them. In fact, by 1994 redfish numbers got so high that TPWD biologists decided it was okay for anglers to harvest a couple of bull redfish each year. TPWD initiated a special red drum "trophy tag."

Fast forward to the 2000s. Now, redfish are super abundant with record numbers reported in bay systems along the Gulf Coast. Anglers are enjoying a redfish renaissance of sorts.

But there are reasons to be concerned.

For example there is a contingent of anglers in Louisiana who say redfish are responsible for causing severe declines in the number and average size of blue crabs in the marshes of Louisiana. I am sure it is not the hundreds of thousands of crab traps in their marshes. It must be the redfish, right?

An official with LDWF who requested anonymity pointed out that commercial crabbers have brought the redfish up on several occasions and have managed to get the attention of high-ranking legislators: "You would thing such statements would be laughed off, but there are actually a few legislators taking this stuff seriously. Actually, the word is that some of them are just looking for any excuse to make the redfish a commercial species. There's a strong movement among some of the commercial guys to make this happen, and I would certainly advise recreational anglers interested in the future of this currently magnificent fishery to be on guard. There seems to be something in the cards for commercializing redfish."

Back in 2001, the Red Drum Advisory Panel (RDAP) of the Gulf of

Mexico Fisheries Management Council (GMFMC) asked federal fisheries managers to consider a "limited commercial season" for redfish. They passed on it the first time, but sources say the concept is gaining serious momentum again.

The future of redfish is bright but concerned anglers must stand guard because commercial interests are out to exploit the species.

Before venturing farther into this sea of bureaucracy, let's examine the roles of these agencies.

The GMFMC serves as an advisory panel to the National Marine Fisheries Service (NMFS), which is the federal agency responsible for managing natural resources in federally controlled waters. GMFMC officials come up with regulatory proposals and forward them to NMFS, which makes the final decision.

The RDAP is one of several GMFMC sub-councils that advise on policy. There are similar panels for pelagic species and blue crabs. (The Acronym Club meets each Wednesday at the local VFW hall.) These panels consist of biologists, commercial fishermen, fishing industry retailers, and, usually, at least one token sport angler. Representatives of the sport fishing community mostly regard the panels as dominated by commercial interests.

If this proposal would have been put into place, it would have involved a set overall poundage or trip quota of redfish to be harvested for commercial purposed from Gulf waters. As much as 200,000 pounds of redfish might be

Stocking redfish has been one of the Texas Parks & Wildlife Department's most successful programs.

taken annually over five years.

According to Peter Hood of the GMFMC said, they based the proposal on a lack of knowledge of redfish stocks in the Gulf of Mexico: "Redfish stocks in open waters of the Gulf are sort of like black holes; we don't know much about them. One of the roles of our council and the RDAP is to determine where stocks are healthy or unhealthy. Government officials in various states banned redfish as a commercial species 20 years ago because they were in trouble. In the inland state waters, redfish seem to be recovered, but we just do not know what their status is in the Gulf. This proposal, which is sort of in a state of limbo, was made to help further research of the species."

NMFS and all the other fisheries panels are strapped for cash and do not have the money to do a full-blown redfish population study. The idea behind a "limited commercial season" would be to put scientists aboard the boats to tag and release some of the reds and study other aspects of the populations. "The commercial fleet would essentially be providing the boats and some of the manpower," according to a GMFMC document. The fisheries people would only have to pay for on-board biologist and limited supplies. It would be a cost-saving measure, or at least that is the idea. With snapper and other species like grouper in the spotlight, there's not much funding for redfish."

The document further recommends:

- Scientists need to know the age composition of adult reds in offshore waters.
- The absolute abundance of adult red drum in the Gulf of Mexico needs to be accurately measured.
- Random sampling of the commercial and recreational catches for age composition data is needed.
- Standardized stock assessment methodology needs to be developed that can accept area- (state-) specific data and work with these within the context of a Gulf-wide stock assessment.
- State-specific contributions of red drum to the offshore adult stock need to be determined

• Angler-release and shrimp-trawl by-catch mortality and the ages or lengths of caught and released fish need to be determined.

• The length composition of the commercial catch (if put in place) needs to be measured.

A similar proposal was revised in 2015, once again involving research.

Redfish stocks may indeed be able to sustain a commercial harvest, and to be perfectly fair, those fish do not belong to sport fishermen or anyone else for that matter—they are supposed to be a public resource. On the other hand, sport anglers are the ones who paid for redfish restoration through saltwater stamp sales, and funded massive stocking programs that increased overall numbers of the fish in Texas and elsewhere along the Gulf Coast. Sport fishermen have lived with restrictive redfish limits to help bolster this magnificent fish. The last time the commercial fishermen had a go with redfish, they nearly fished them into oblivion. That is not an opinion, but a documented fact.

These proposals keep popping up but never see the light of day. Numerous other issues are taking up the time and resources of NMFS, and support for redfish conservation is still high among conservation groups and state fish and game agencies

Only time will tell whether we will see another round of the redfish wars that dominated the coastal fishing scene of the 1970's. If the battles do start, hopefully the redfish will come out of the winner once again.

This awesome fish certainly deserves it.

Chapter Fourteen

Miscellaneous Tips, Tactics, and Trivia

FILLETING REDFISH

Redfish have big, tough scales and are tough to clean for some anglers. I always use an electric knife and following technique. Rinse the fish and put it on a fish skinning board that has a clip to hold the tail in place.

With an electric knife, cut the tail near the end down to the vertebrae and stop. Then cut down the length of the vertebrae all the way up to the gills. Make sure and leave behind a little thin layer of meat so you do not get bone with the fillet.

Next, cut the fillet from the tip of the gills area downward. Remove the fish from the clip and clip on the fillet. Cut down the length of the fillet, hugging the inside skin of the scale side with the blade.

Repeat the process with fish on the other side.

You might lose a little meat doing it this way, but it is much faster than any other method I have tried.

PROPER FILLET KNIFE USAGE

Texas Fish and Game magazine reader Don Collins sent in this tip.

When filleting or cleaning different fish, you'll probably have to cut through some fairly heavy bone at some stage. To do this safely and effectively, never use your good filleting knife on bone. They have fairly pliable steel blades and can flex, causing them to slip off the bone and into the person doing the job. It will also blunt the edge, requiring more frequent sharpening, plus it will needlessly wreck your good blade over time. When cutting through bone, use a heavy-duty blade with a good sharp edge, and never cut towards yourself.

PHOTO BY GRADY ALLEN

The electric knife is an indispensable tool for any angler serious about eating fish.

LINE TWIST PROBLEMS

Line twist is almost unavoidable because it is caused by so many factors. Lures that twist, such as plastic worms with hooks off-center, spoons, and spinners, are common causes. You can also twist a line with a spinning or spin-casting reel when you continue to turn the handle while a fish is taking out line. Every turn of the rotor puts a full twist in the line.

No matter what causes the twist, it is easy to remove, according to the experts at Stren. They suggest you remove all terminal tackle from the line and troll the bare line behind your boat for a few minutes. The current running over the line quickly takes out the twist.

APPROACH ROUGH WATER WITH CAUTION

If you have been fishing for long at all, you have been caught in rough water, or will soon. One thing you will quickly learn is to take big waves one at a time. Each wave is just a little different, so you usually have to handle each one a little differently.

Sometimes, there may seem to be a rhythm to the waves, but you still have to study each one because a bigger wave may be coming up behind the smaller ones. If you are not alert, you can and will get your buns soaked in a hurry, or worse.

One way to navigate big waves is to slow your boat. Many anglers try to run rough water excessively fast because they want to get to safety as quickly as possible. If you take waves too fast, you may take water on board and possibly swamp.

Most of experienced boaters power up the face of a wave, then slow down as they go back down and accelerate up the next wave. You have to keep the nose of the boat up or you will cut right through a wave and take on water.

Sometimes it is possible to run between the waves, taking each wave at a slight angle. This method can result in staying in rough water longer, but it may be the safest method to use.

Confidence in your experience is another major factor in learning to successfully navigate rough water. None of us enjoys being caught in conditions that could be potentially life threatening. Knowing that you are capable of navigating to safety really gives you better judgment.

Today's boat manufacturers have made handling rough water a lot easier by building longer and wider boats. The extra length and width add greatly to your safety.

Always think safety and common sense when fishing from a boat. Your life, or your partner's, could depend on your judgment.

MULTIPLE HOOK-UP TIPS

When saltwater fishing, multiple hook-ups occur frequently, and many times the fish are the same weight class. When two big ones hook up at the

Catching redfish is fun but anglers need to keep safety in mind-especially when wade fishing or as I have experience-being hooked up with multiple fish. Angler Marcus Heflin pictured here has probably caught more redfish in the surf than anyone in the state in the last 20 years.

same time, let one fish run against a little drag on it and separate it from the other one. Letting the fish stay together is asking for tangled lines as well as one or both fish being lost. Fight them one at a time for the best results.

REDFISH HOOKING TIPS

While fishing for bull redfish, most of what you catch will be released, so you must start using circle hooks. They always hook in the mouth and rarely gut hook. They are the best hooks for cut bait, live bait, and dead bait.

A good tip when baiting up with these hooks is to tie a knot tight on the bottom of the shank of the hook, using about 30-pound-test monofilament. This will keep the bait from sliding up the hook.

Also try mashing down the barb, you will be surprised that you just do not need it.

REDFISH FICTION

One book in a children's nature series by author Suzanne Tate is titled *Old Reddy Drum: A Tale of Redfish.* The publisher describes it: "Old Reddy Drum, a wise and powerful fish, gives life-saving advice to a young Peter Puppy Drum."

A HERO NAMED "REDFISH"

The image of big bull red rising to attack a topwater plug must have inspired U.S. Navy brass in WWII, for one of the most famous of the submarine fleet was christened *USS Redfish.*

The Portsmouth Navy Yard in Portsmouth, New Hampshire, laid her keel 9 September 1943, and launched her 27 January 1944 as part of the largest single-day launch of U.S. subs during WWII.

Redfish had an overall length of 311 feet, 6 inches; an extreme beam of 27 feet, 3 inches; a standard displacement of 1526 tons; a mean draft of 15 feet, 3 inches; and a submerged displacement of 2,391 tons. Her surface speed was 20.25 knots, submerged speed 8.25 knots. She had a design depth of 400 feet.

On one of its first Pacific patrols in the war with Japan, *Redfish* headed for Saipan teamed with *Sea Devil.* On the night of 8-9 December, the pair put Japanese aircraft carrier *Junyo* out of commission for the rest of the war. Dodging past escorts, *Redfish* made three separate attacks until the heavily damaged

Junyo passed through the barrier of the Nagasaki minefields. Though not sunk, the carrier was damaged beyond repair.

The Japanese Imperial Navy sent another carrier to the Philippines, newly built *Unryu*, an 18,500-ton vessel rushed south by way of the East China Sea—more fodder for the mighty *Redfish* and its crew.

On the afternoon of 19 December, *Redfish* spotted a fast destroyer on the horizon, and an aircraft dropped a depth charge. A second destroyer soon appeared, then a Japanese carrier cleared the horizon and zigzagged toward the submarine. *Redfish* did not even have to alter course during her attack approach. Within eight minutes, four bow torpedoes struck and stopped *Unryu* dead in the water. The carrier opened up with all her starboard side guns while *Redfish* let go with four more torpedoes at an escort destroyer, which had passed just astern. The destroyer turned away from the torpedo wakes.

Shells and depth charges exploded at random while *Redfish* worked feverishly to reload. One steam torpedo aimed just aft of the carrier island brought thunderous secondary detonations from deep in *Unryu's* bowels. Clouds of smoke, flame, and debris enveloped the enemy carrier. *Redfish* dove to escape the fury of the destroyers—and "all hell broke loose."

Seven well-placed depth charges exploded alongside the starboard bow as *Redfish* passed 150 feet. Her steering gear jammed hard left. There was a hydraulic leak in the manifold, her bow planes jammed on 20 degrees up bevel, and loss of all hydraulic power. All sonar was off-line, and the pressure hull cracked in the forward torpedo room. There were numerous air leaks throughout the submarine, and a torpedo was making a hot run in the No. 8 tube.

The submarine came to rest in 232 feet of water, secured all running machinery, and waited out her pursuers. In a little more than two hours, *Redfish* was on the surface and running away from the destroyers at flank speed. The *Unryu* lay on the bottom along with her crated cargo of 30 experimental kamikaze rocket-bombs.

Redfish proceeded to Pearl Harbor, then to San Francisco, and later through the Panama Canal to Portsmouth Naval Shipyard. Her battle damage was repaired by 2 July, and she again sailed for Pacific combat. She arrived at Pearl Harbor on 22 July and was preparing for a third patrol when the "end of hostilities" came on 15 August 1945. Two days later, *Redfish* was presented with the Presidential Unit Citation for extraordinary heroism in action during her two war patrols. *Redfish* was also two Battle Stars for her actions.

After the war, the proud submarine served in training, intelligence, and special ops roles. Equipped with an experimental fathometer and a powerful underwater light, on 23 August 1952 *Redfish* became the first American submarine to operate an extended mission beneath the Arctic Ice, paving the way for a new era in submarine deployment. This adventure nearly ended in disaster as *Redfish* found herself trapped in a pack of drifting floes and heading toward "hostile waters." Redfish battled her way at conning tower depth back through the heavy seas of the Bering Straits and limped home to Pearl Harbor with damage to both screws and minus her torpedo tube doors.

The submarine's "special ops" included movie appearances. In 1954, *Redfish* starred in the Walt Disney production of Jules Verne's *20,000 Leagues Under The Sea.* Movie grips fitted her with a dummy rear fin for to mimic Capt. Nemo's *Nautilus* in one of the most dramatic sequences in the film.

In September 1957 *Redfish* starred as the *USS Nerka* in the MGM submarine classic, *Run Silent, Run Deep.* She finished her film career with several appearances in the popular black-and-white television series, "Silent Service."

After a long and distinguished career that included live saving and counter espionage missions, the aging *Redfish* was decommissioned in San Diego on 27 June 1968, her name struck from the Navy List 30 June 1968. Her stripped hull, like those of many sister vessels, was used for fleet target practice and sunk off the Pacific Coast. One of her former crewman described it as "a sad but fitting end for a brave fighting submarine."

Chapter Fifteen
Wade-fishing

Sometimes, it simply pays to get in the water with redfish. This is an especially good method when a falling tide reveals redfish actively feeding in the shallows with their tails or dorsal fins sticking out of the water. This allows for the exciting possibility of sight-casting.

More than a decade ago, my good friend, Lee Leschper, wrote an excellent article for *Texas Fish & Game* magazine called "Beginner's Guide to Wade-fishing." The basics covered in that article are still relevant today, so I thought it would be an appropriate beginning to this chapter. Here it is, with permission.

> The last shrimp went the way of the quart of his predecessors—one jiggle of the popping cork, and a swarm of pinfish ripped it to shreds.
>
> Aching back and scorching sun pointed me toward the shoreline, a sloshing, thigh-deep, half-mile away. A single "barely" redfish followed me on a long stringer. I was

burnt, parched, and salty as a 30-day ham.

I was in heaven.

Wade-fishing is the best way to catch trophy-sized Texas speckled trout and redfish. It is a cheap, easy alternative to boats and gas bills. It is also salve for the nerves, food for the spirit, and refresher for the soul.

Sadly, millions of Texans still imagine that saltwater angling always involves huge boats, winch-like tackle, and the constant threat of seasickness.

That is just not so.

Our favorite bay sport fish, the speckled trout and redfish, are shallow water denizens. They live, feed, and breed on the clear sand and salt grass flats. These flats, back bays, bayous, and estuaries are the richest waters on the coast, home to every conceivable form of fish and crustacean life, including the shrimp, crabs, mullet, pinfish, and croakers that game fish love.

Many of these flats are less than knee deep and too shallow for all but the shallowest running tunnel hull boats. In this skinny water, any boat traffic will spook the wary fish. Even a drifting boat throws a big shadow and a big profile across the flats.

A wade-fisherman, on the other hand, is silent and almost invisible. He can slip undetected to within feet of big trout. That is why many of the best guides on the coast—driving the best shallow-water boats money can buy—still wade-fish. All the state record speckled trout fell to waders.

This is fishing stripped down to its essence—man vs. fish, in the fish's world. Tackle is likewise pared down to the basics:

• One trusted graphite rod—a 7-foot popping rod and casting reel or similar spinning tackle. Load the casting reel with 12-pound-test Berkley Big Game, the spinning reel with 10-pound-test Stren.

• Spare lures, including gold spoons, D.O.A. shrimp or mullet imitations, Cocahoe Minnows or Salty Assassins, and a few broken-back or Top Dog topwaters.

• Twenty-pound-test leader material.

• Popping corks or rattling floats.

• Floating bait bucket and No. 6 treble hooks for live shrimp and 2/0 Kahle hooks for live croaker or mullet.

• Small pocket tackle box.

• Needle-nose pliers.

• Saltwater stringer with a healthy float at one end.

• Landing net (optional).

Travel light, but prepared. It's a long walk back if you lose the only bait that works. Your favorite bass rod will probably work just fine. Just remember that longer casts are important here, so lighter line and a longer rod yield more distance. Casting tackle is my favorite, but if you can get more distance from a spinning rig, use it. Most of the guides on the lower coast use spinning tackle.

Add a 2- to 3-foot shock leader of 20-pound mono at the end of the line to combat sharp teeth and abrasive shell. The reel should hold plenty of line and have a butter-smooth drag. This is no place to scrimp on quality. Saltwater is as corrosive as acid and will destroy cheap reels in no time. At the end of each day, wash your gear in freshwater and spray it with a lubricant like Corrosion X.

Remember that the wind usually blows on the

coast. Wade downwind so you can always cast with the wind at your back. It will add 30 feet to your casts and eliminate backlashes.

A gold 1/4- or 1/2-ounce weedless spoon has to be the No. 1 lure on the flats. Add half of a strawberry tout for more buoyancy in shallow water. A spoon has lots of lift, and fished with high rod tip can slip along nicely in 6 inches of water. Lift the bait slightly with the rod tip, reel a foot or so, pause, and lift again.

Just as effective are the soft plastic shrimp and fish imitations. The Cocahoe Queen and Salty Assassin baits both imitate finger mullet and are superb wading baits. Rig them on the lightest jighead you can cast, and retrieve them with that same start and stop retrieve. You can seldom go wrong with red-and-white, avocado metal-flake, chartreuse, and pumpkin pepper patterns. The D.O.A. shrimp and mullet imitations are equally deadly; inventor Mark Nichols blended natural shape and action into deadly baits.

There is no dishonor in using live bait. Fish live shrimp 18 to 30 inches under a popping cork, just deep enough to reach the bottom. Hook the shrimp on a No. 6 treble hook just under the horn at the end of its nose and gently lob it out. Jerking the cork through the water like a topwater bass lure simulates the sound of fish feeding, attracting competitive trout. The cadence for popping the cork is a very personal, almost mystical matter. Some pop to the rhythm of songs such as "Happy Birthday" and "Mary had a Little Lamb." You want to pop just enough to attract attention without scaring away everything on the flat.

Live shrimp can be hard to find, especially late in

the summer or on a busy weekend, and cost $8 to $10 a quart. They are hard to keep alive, but they work.

Live croaker and finger mullet are great baits for big trout and reds. These tough baits live longer and are not bothered much by trash fish. Hook croaker and mullet through the back just under the dorsal fin on a 2-0 Kahle hook. Then lob them unweighted into one of the creamy white potholes of bare sand you see out on the grass flats. Any red or trout in the area will nail it. Because of the size of these baits, you have to give the game fish time to get the bait into its mouth.

The key to whipping a fish on the flats is letting it run freely against light drag until it tires. Pre-set the drag just heavy enough to set the hook, and no more. Keep the rod tip high and let the drag and bend of the rod do the work. Wear the fish down before trying to net or grab it—a "green" red can wrap you in a cocoon of your own line. If you are keeping fish, string it before you unhook it.

When landing fish, grab them around the head at the base of the gills. Most saltwater game fish have sharp teeth so you cannot lip-land them.

Summer wading in Texas does not require fancy waders; old jeans and long-sleeved shirt or a light cotton one-piece jumpsuit work fine. Shorts are comfortable but do not provide protection from jellyfish. Old sneakers are the traditional footwear, but neoprene wading shoes are infinitely more comfortable and durable. The stingray-proof booties are even better.

Wear a long-sleeve shirt and cover all exposed skin with a good sunscreen. A long-billed cap is mandatory.

Good polarized sunglasses are essential, both to protect your eyes and to help you see fish in the clear water of the flats.

There are more than 300 miles of shallow bays along the Texas coast and almost all offer productive wade-fishing, if you know what to look for. Trout and reds always follow the baitfishes. Look for flats with clear water and baitfishes, especially schools of mullet. Look for "nervous" water rippling with finger mullet or mullet jumping out of the water. Use you eyes and nose to locate oily, watermelon-smelling slicks made by feeding trout.

Sand and grass bottom is better than mud. Oyster shell draws fish, but is brutal on the ankles. A broad shallow flat adjacent to deeper water, whether the Intracoastal Canal or deeper bay waters, is always a good bet. Flats near a pass (a channel connecting the bay to the Gulf of Mexico) or between a main bay and smaller secondary bay are always productive at some time during the day.

Early and late in the day, game fish move shallower. They follow tides any time of day. High tide, when water is moving into the flats and carrying bait with it, is the best time to fish shallower.

Low tides, when the water is moving out, are best for fishing deeper flats, or the passes themselves. As the summer heats up, fish move deep earlier in the day, so be on the flats at first light.

Boat traffic drives fish deeper, but undisturbed redfish may be in shin-deep water anytime of day. Keep moving and looking. If one flat is barren of bait and game fish, don't waste time there.

> Even if the fish evade you, the waters will embrace you like a mother finding a lost child. The gentle waves and singing breeze, the skittering baitfish and scuttling crabs, the gulls laughing overhead and the taste and smell of salt will take root in your soul.

GEARING UP

As Lee pointed out, while wading for reds, it is important to wear the proper attire and that starts with good footwear. Proper wade-fishing footwear completely covers and protects your feet from shells and other harmful objects. I often use old sneakers, partly because I am cheap, and partly because they work just fine. Numerous companies make wade-fishing booties designed specifically for this purpose. I am partial to the "Water Tennies" made by the Five Ten company. They have a neoprene mesh top and a hard rubber bottom. This allows the foot to breathe a little but at the same time gives solid protection. I use these during the late spring and early summer and then switch to my old sneakers worn over neoprene waders in fall and winter.

During winter months, neoprene waders are must-have. Catching redfish is cool and everything, but hypothermia is not. Waders are also good for protecting against stingrays and other hazards, which we will get to later. Nowadays, I wade-fish with a life vest on and consider it a necessary tool in the wade-fishing game. Yes, most of the time you will be wading in shallow water, but many things can happen. The tide could pull you into deep water, or the wake of a ship thrown onto the flats from a ship channel could knock you back. Then again, it could pull you toward it.

Wading belts are a must-have item because they allow you to carry everything from pliers to lures while fishing. More importantly, they give you back support, which is very important in wade-fishing. A day wading can be hell on the lower back, so you need all the support you can get.

I own good wading belts and recommend both. The Wade-Aid also serves as a floating device, although not Coast Guard certified, and is good for an added safety measure.

I carry a little homemade strap on tackle box that holds a half-dozen hard lures, has a compartment for plastics and jigheads, and strap for my needle-nose pliers. There are lots of wading gear boxes on the market. Some are good and some are junk. My best recommendation is to use a small, light box and carry as few lures as you can get away with.

STINGRAYS

Stingrays are the single greatest threat to wade-fishermen. Although not a vicious animal by nature, it can inflict severe pain with its "barbed" stinger if a wader steps on it. The best way to avoid a stingray hit is to shuffle your feet while wading. Many anglers call this the "stingray shuffle," and while it may feel silly, it can save you a lot of trouble and an expensive hospital bill.

While wade-fishing the Chandeleur Islands in 1998, I waded out from an island back to our boat. Just as I was about to step into the boat, I noticed a massive ray right in front of my foot. Had I been stepping, I would have been on my way to the hospital. But because I was shuffling, the big, ugly thing scooted in the other direction.

As many anglers on the coast of Florida say: "Keep your feet on the bottom."

Something to keep in mind is that most stingrays are invisible to the naked eye. They are masters of camouflage and can be under your feet without you ever knowing. If you see a few rays around, there is a good chance there are dozens or maybe hundreds in the vicinity. To counter this potential threat, some companies now produce stingray shields and stingray proof boots. Some anglers feel they are too cumbersome to wear, but I have a feeling those who have been hit by rays would disagree.

Anglers wanting to keep fish will have to invest in either a floating stringer or a floating ring with a fish basket. I advise using the latter because sharks love to attack fish on stringers. Sometimes they will hit the baskets, too, but your chances of an encounter with "Jaws" will greatly decrease.

Perhaps even more important than what type of device you will use to keep the fish on is how long the rope is. I now go with a 35-foot rope to attach my float ring to the wading belt. An encounter with a big shark in the Chandeleur Islands got me to wanting my fish as far away from me as I can get them. In case you have not noticed, that area is very wild and untamed with lots of potential dangers. The fishing there is magnificent, so the ends justify the means.

And that is sort of the theme with wade-fishing, because it is not for everyone. If you have never seriously pursued wade-fishing, you might consider it strange to soak oneself in saltwater and deal with possible encounters with hazards like stingrays when boats offer more comfort and allow you to cover more ground more quickly. But that is exactly what dedicated waders do not like.

From my standpoint, I see stealth as a very important aspect of wading. Because walking in saltwater can be flat-out tough, wading forces the angler to fish slower and look at an area differently.

Being in a more intimate relationship with your surroundings creates a different perspective, and sometimes, that is what it takes to get anglers to see the little things that can lead to limits of reds.

Thanks and Acknowledgments

Writing a book is vastly different than any other kind of creative endeavor.

Books are often snapshots of our lives as much as they are exposes on a particular topic. What is going on in our lives will reflect at least in the tone of the book. A book is like a journey across life highlighted by what's going on in the author's life at the time of writing.

The first edition of Texas Reds was written during a very dark period of my life. Professionally things were great but on a personal note I was struggling with anger and was about to come to a major life-altering crossroads.

Shortly after the book came out, I made a decision to invite Jesus Christ back into my life as Lord and Savior and my life has slowly but radically changed since then.

When I had an opportunity to do an expanded edition, I was excited.

While I stand by the first edition and have had many people share how much they enjoyed it I believe after looking I could have pushed even deeper into the topic.

And that is what you get here.

I never write just basic how-to fishing books.

My works are done how I think which is definitely not the norm in terms of fishing or hunting. I like to take a wholistic approach to the outdoors and teach as much about the ecosystem and the life habits of the fish or game as which hooks or bullets to use.

This edition goes much deeper into that realm and also updates things like preferred lures and tactics. It's got a highly uplifting tone as well as how to pattern trophy redfish in ways that I never understood back when the first edition came out. In fact, the strategies for trophy reds listed here have never been written about this way by anyone as far as I know.

I have spent a vast amount of time pursuing giant reds along the Gulf Coast since then and in the F.L.E.X. Fishing chapter show you how to virtually guarantee catching the biggest red of your life.

I have always been honest with readers and shared facts few in my profession dare mention. I have never been shy about admitting things like getting invited on awesome fishing trips because I'm a writer and getting free gear to fish with. It drives me nuts when I see others being asked what gear they recommend and they go to some super high-end equipment only because someone is giving it to them. I may recommend some of that stuff too because it's good but always say "but if you can't afford this here are other options."

I am only in this position by the grace of God and never take it for granted. And I don't take you for granted either, remembering the days when I could only afford to fish from the side of the road sitting on a white bucket.

When I have been able to travel the world fishing I remember those days and appreciate the journey and never forget where I came from.

Now it's time for the thanks…

I would like to thank the Lord Jesus Christ for loving and forgiving me and for continually renewing me.

Thanks to my wife Lisa for being just flat out amazing and being there for everything I have ever done in this career. I love you more today than I did when we first got married-and that was a lot!

To my daughter Faith for making me smile every day. I love you sweetheart.

To my mom Gloria for always supporting me and being the best grandmother ever and to my late father Chester Moore, Sr. for taking me out and letting me catch my first redfish on the side of Highway 87 between Bridge City and Port Arthur.

To my and Lisa's spiritual daughter Demi Schlageter. We love you and are proud of who you are who you are becoming.

To Reannah Hollaway for showing me what it's like to be a fighter and for your heart for wildlife conservation.

To Todd and Annie Jurasek for helping steer me toward Christ and always being there in more ways than anyone else ever has outside of my wife and parents. I love you more than you know.

To Mike Williams for being such a good friend and always being there for our ministry.

Thanks to Roy and Ardia Neves for believing me in early on and allowing me to take an unorthodox approach to the great outdoors. I am blessed to be Editor-In-Chief of Texas Fish & Game.

And to everyone who has helped my career in any way. There are too many of you to mention. Thank you all.

And a Chester Moore book wouldn't be a Chester Moore book without mentioning my pop culture inspirations during this time.

Thanks to the late great Stan Lee for teaching me about alliteration (I use it all the time in story titles) and showing me that imagination can give you a career. My life wouldn't be as enjoyable without Spider Man, The Incredible Hulk, the X-Men and the rest of your creations.

Thanks to the Young Bucks, Kenny Omega, Cody Rhodes and the rest of The Elite for showing through pro wrestling that people who do things for the love of it can reinvent not only themselves but an entire industry.

And finally, thanks to all of you who read my work, listen to my broadcasts and attend my lectures. I greatly appreciate you.

Now, go catch some redfish!

Index

F

H

I

J

K

L

M

T

U

V

W

www.ingramcontent.com/pod-product-compliance
Lightning Source LLC
LaVergne TN
LVHW020715110826
845149LV00012B/2272
* 9 7 8 0 9 9 0 8 4 1 5 2 4 *